Americans the Beautiful

Theresa Tsai Liu

authorHOUSE®

AuthorHouse™
1663 Liberty Drive
Bloomington, IN 47403
www.authorhouse.com
Phone: 1 (800) 839-8640

Published by AuthorHouse 10/02/2017

ISBN: 978-1-5462-0832-7 (sc)
ISBN: 978-1-5462-0831-0 (e)

Contents

Acknowledgements

Stories are told based on viewpoints. A single incident may happen, but, our recounting is enhanced through nuances and perspectives shaped by the life we have lived and the influences that have driven us forward.

In my life, I have been blessed with the wonderful insights and thoughts of people close to me. I appreciate them all. Preparing this book, I realized how important and beautiful you are to me.

Thank you to my three grade school classmates. When we reconnected in 2011, I saw the brilliance and strength of characteristics that have withstood the tests of time and life. The longer and further you go, the more you see the value of home. We recognize and cherish our deep-rooted, traditional Chinese heritage and values – family, friendship, respect, leadership, education, and appreciation. You are like family. My thanks to *Charles Cha, Steven Chen, and James Huang.*

My deepest gratitude to my American friends. They are the stars of these stories. For me, you provide the inspiration and themes so important to writing these portraits: *Brother Joe, Dave Murphy, Steve Novack, Dr.Jeffrey Marsh, Dr. Lisa, Dr. Greg, Kim Furlow, Steve Hilton, Kent Burgess, Abraham Mohler, Joey Ruzicka, Billy Foster, Kath Kuper, Mark Lee, Katherine Dowling, Mandy Ruzicka, Tauriana King, Jayne Baulos, Craig Fenner, Donna Pelikan, Mike Holdinghaus, Sarah Yancey* and *Dr. Martin Bell.* Thank you for showing and sharing how you applied yourself to achieve wonderful dreams for humanity, creativity, entrepreneurship, independence and inspiration.

Warmest thanks to my editor, **David Murphy**, who helped build these stories with editing that cleaned up grammar. Our cultural discussions along with experiments over wontons helped create the stories that fill these stories. Thank you for understanding and building a strong cultural knowledge that you can pass to your two daughters adopted from China.

Through thick and thin, through work and life challenges, **Donna Pelikan** has been there to help me steer through good times and hard. When we taught together for 10 years, Donna opened my eyes and heart to new ideas. I admire Donna for actively involved with organization - Reading Success Center since she retired. My deep appreciation and thanks to your dedication to reading program in St. Louis.

True friends help you with truth. The greatest friendships can be characterized by the ability to tell it like it is. As I was going through these stories, I shared them with friends and the truth! Thank you to **Kim Resis, Linda Lanham, Amy Baum, Starr Braun-Huon, Judy Goldammer, Jayne Baker, Sue McHugh,** and **Becky Cornel** and **Myra Klahr** for you made these stores better, just as you have always made my life even better through your friendship.

How do you honor and show admiration for a man who feeds the homeless, helps the elderly, reaches out to young people in need? I give the gift of stories that touch others. To **Steve Ruzicka**, who stays in my heart and my mind, I share these stories that only touch on the characteristics that I have seen in you all these years. You are a genuine hero. Humble as you may be, please know that your actions are recognized and admired. Thank you.

One Chinese proverb said the best:
* *Life is partly what we make it, and partly what is is made by the friends whom we choose.*

To my daughter, **Helen**, I love you more than any book could ever capture. You are my supportive, intelligent, beautiful, nurturing and lovely one. If you could see into my heart, you would see the glow and love that I feel for you. You, my cherished one, carry the most beautiful parts of life and share them with others. Thank you for being you. I am proud of you. You are my sunshine, my only sunshine.

Family is very important to me. My family values are at the core of these stories and have served as a beacon guiding my entire life. My brothers and sisters have always been my ground force. One in Paris and three in San Francisco, my siblings still remind me of the importance of education, family, and Chinese culture. Because of our father died young, we found comfort, and direction from and with each other while our mother found solace in the church. Led by my oldest brother, **Foch,** we all stayed close and supportive as we all came to the USA to study at graduate school and start our careers, families and adult lives.

For the happiness, inspiration, comfort and caring, I thank and love each and every one of my siblings from the bottom of my heart: *Foch, MIng-ming, David and Lulu.*

Foreword

There are people who come in to your life at critical moments. In the ebb and flow of human existence, we all gain and lose perspective on the most important parts of life. Family. Loved ones. Charity. Passion. Compassion. These concepts are fully comprehensible, but the true gifts and nature of these potent forces shall be cherished and acknowledged.

There were times in my life when I have lost perspective. The churn of work and activities, the chase of the mighty dollar to obtain the latest gadget, the chase of most anything that is truly fleeting or insubstantial usually can only create empty wins. These were rewards without staying power.

Several years ago, through a series of circumstances, I met Theresa Liu. Her spirit, enthusiasm and energy are immediately present. But, deeper down, there was the experience and perspective that builds connections. She may never know the full extent of it, but she popped into my life when I was at a crossroads. Her thoughts and perspectives are still helping to shine a way forward as I move on my path.

These pages ahead of you share stories of people. Many of these people you have not met. You may never meet. For Theresa, her gift is the beautiful art of sharing and impressing the meaning of the people.

Dozens of people may describe a flower. Yet, for all of us, there are but a few who can truly capture and share the spirit, aroma, and aesthetic of the bloom. We all observe and can describe. The true gift is in the ability to connect with others on the impression any feature may deliver.

Theresa's sense of people and the way they interact with others is a rare one. Read these stories and feel the way these wonderful, complex, creative, and beautiful people come to life. The subject in a photograph is the second most important part of creating the art. The photographer's sense and sensibility are foremost.

See the brightness and alluring elegance from the eyes of Theresa Liu. Read with pleasure and see things from a new point of view.

David Murphy

The Last Generation of Chinese Mainlanders

Theresa Liu

My siblings and grade school classmates were born in the 1940's during the chaotic civil war in China; we followed our parents and moved to Taiwan. The native Taiwanese referred to us as "inlanders," but, we call ourselves "mainlanders." While we were growing up in Taiwan, our parents encouraged us to go to America where there were more opportunities. At that time, the only way we were allowed to enter America was to pursue higher education. So, we all diligently studied hard from elementary school to college and came to United States for advanced study in order to build a strong and steady career.

My generation were all born in mainland China, raised in Taiwan, now have all lived in the United States for fifty years, three very different cultures in one life! We call ourselves the last generation of Chinese Mainlanders even as we wholeheartedly treasure our family and friendship in this land of opportunity - USA.

Falling Leaves Return to Their Roots 落葉歸根

We were too young to remember the refugee years from China to Taiwan. Now, at retirement age, we get together whenever and wherever we have the chance. Each time when we reunite either as family or as a class, the famous Chinese proverb 'Falling Leaves Return to Their Roots' (落葉歸根) always comes to my mind. This old Chinese saying refers to people who are at the end of their journey, as they grow old, searching for the "origin," they decide to seek their "roots" in their hometown. Each time when I meet up with my siblings or old classmates, from New York, Missouri, or California, we still speak in Mandarin, think like Chinese and act like Chinese even though we all have resided in America for five decades.

One day, out of blue, I got a phone call from my grade school classmate Charles Cha. I was speechless! No, actually I was screaming! Before the phone call, I had not heard nor seen any one from that class, the class of **Trust**, after the graduation. Over the phone, Charles excitedly asked me to join the upcoming class reunion in Los Angeles. That phone call has enriched my retirement life more joyful and meaningful! That was the year of 2011.

Our group of elementary classmates graduated from the same school; we all stayed in the same classroom, from 8 am to 4 pm, every single day for six years in Taipei, Taiwan. Our bonds are solid and our friendships are pure. After each class reunion, I always conclude that my generation has inherited our deep-rooted, traditional, Chinese heritage and values. But, we have also learned to appreciate the American culture and spirit.

At my very first grade school class reunion in July of 2011, we gathered at a LA Chinese restaurant where I met my literally "old" friends for the first time in fifty years! The feeling of exuberance was overpowering to me; there was no one single appropriate word to describe the moment. We were literally screaming with joy! I recognized some of them immediately and for others, I only remembered their names. Nevertheless, through our exhilarated greetings to each other and recalling the innocent days at grade school years, all of us shared fond memories about Charles during our grade school years.

Charles Cha, Natural Leader, 尊師重道

It all began in 2007, Charles had the idea to reunite our classmates; he started to search through social media to locate everyone, one by one till in July 2011 when he found me. Since then, I have joined the reunions from California to Missouri.

I remembered during our grade school years, Charles listened when we talked during the breaks; he comforted the "misbehaved" classmates who were reprimanded by teachers or standing alone in the hallway as punitive treatment by authority figures; he frequently invited the boys to ride bikes with him after school; he treated friends to watch free movies at the theater since his father owned the movie company.

After my very first class reunion, Charles invited all of us to meet again, as usual, but he also invited our home room teacher and her husband. Both were in their late 80's and living in Pittsburgh. They even accepted the invitation to join future reunions: one on a cruise ship and another one in Minnesota. Charles collected the financial support from the classmates for the expenses of these trips for both of them. Last year, he learned that Teacher Liu had fallen down a staircase and Charles asked us to comfort her with phone calls and flowers. When I asked him the reason, Charles response was:

"During the 4th and 5th grades, we changed home room teachers several times and our class was on the edge of collapsing without the adequate leadership. As a result, we were not doing our best until Teacher Liu showed up. She definitely had a positive impact on us so that we were able to learn and graduate. We all should show our gratitude to her guidance during our troubled time."

Charles' recollection of that troubled time in our grade school years suddenly helped me to understand why my parents pulled me out of that class and transferred me to another class at the beginning of my 6th grade. Charles, the natural leader was only in his preteen age. Because I moved on to another class in the same school, I lost out on Charles' leadership.

In 2016, ten elementary school classmates gathered in Las Vegas. Charles called Teacher Liu before the celebration dinner started. We wanted to honor her. Each of us took turns speaking with our homeroom teacher over the phone. Teacher Liu, now in her 90's, was delighted and very touched by this gesture.

Education has always been a highly valued trait as we grew up. Respecting authority figures such as parents, teachers, leader and elderly figures has been one of our major cultural characteristics. Charles himself not only was the class leader at our grade school but even now he still is a role model for us because the quality of leadership. He thoughtfully plans out each gathering by giving all considerations where and how to meet and where to spend the night as well as what activities we should do. I have noticed that we all still show respect to his decision making. He himself advanced his career by earning Ph.D in physics at the University of Missouri in Columbia. He had years of successful career in the field working at companies specializing in ultrasonics, robotics and factory automation until he retired about ten years ago. Still a leader, he shows his skills and acumen in many ways including reconnecting old friends.

Recently, Charles revealed his motivation for the class reunions to me when I asked.

"After retirement, I just started to miss this most innocent, carefree and happy period of my life and my classmates..."

Steve Chen, Generous Donor, 飲水思源

Steve and I didn't recognize each other when we met at my first class reunion. Yet, he and his beautiful wife, Bess, graciously invited me to stay at their Los Angeles house. At his home and during the reunion, Steve Chen and I found out we shared many things in common. We are both the middle child of 5 siblings and we both lost our fathers when we were young. Surprisingly, we both learned to play the harmonica for pleasure. I can play simple, playful songs in C major, whereas he can play 3 harmonicas simultaneously and plays classical music. I was in awe of his musical talents and his extreme humanity. My admiration grew to the highest notes. I found out that behind his humble appearance, he was CEO of his company. His deep-rooted Chinese sense of gratitude was beyond belief. I learned that he treated all of his employees and their spouses to cruise ship vacations. This was the first time I had known a boss who is so generous and cares so much about his employees. When I asked him the reason, his answer was:

"Family is important! On the cruise ship, they could enjoy their coworkers and families in a relaxed atmosphere and got to know each other. No need to worry about other stuff... I am grateful for their hard work and support! I don't want to take their hard work for granted."

Ten years ago, Steve needed a kidney transplant. Anxiously waiting for the right one, he and his wife even traveled to a foreign country. Unexpectedly, he was informed that they found a perfect match in the United States so they flew back to America. The perfect match was from a young American guy who died in car accident. After the successful transplant, Steve and Bess were determined to find the donor. Due to medical confidentiality restrictions, it took them nearly five years to locate the donor's family in the New Jersey farmland.

Steve and Bess flew to New Jersey to express their sincere gratitude in person to the donor's mother. During that visit, they learned their donor had two nephews who were toddlers. Steve and Bess presented a promise to set up educational funds for the nephews. Since then, they also keep in touch with the donor's family by visiting them each year and making monthly phone calls.

In 2015, during our class reunion, as usual, seven of us were invited to stay at Steve's San Francisco house. Being a gracious Chinese hostess, Bess prepared homemade Chinese food for everyone. One morning, she was on the phone talking with the donor's mother while making breakfast for us. This time, her tone was concerned. Bess was worried because the donor's mother now had cancer. She comforted the donor's mother over the phone. Steve and Bess have extended their warm hearts and feeling to supporting her financially and ease the burden of her medical expenses. What touched my soul was what Steve said to me:

"*Be always grateful for people's sacrifice. Like our Chinese proverb says that **if you drink the water, don't forget who dug the well.** Personally, I thank them from the bottom of my heart, but for her and her son, my heart has no bottom.*"

It seems to me that their gratitude is real when they express it. Reserving a feeling of gratitude without a related act is like wrapping a present and not giving it. To all Chinese, gratitude is the memory of the heart.

At reunion, Steve always invites our group to stay at his house either Minnesota, San Francisco or Los Angeles. He always volunteers to drive us in his van from city to city, and Bess makes Chinese breakfasts, lunches and dinner for us. Steve is a generous donor who "serves" us in every way he can.

James Huang, Little Grass, 小草

The very first time I saw James at our reunion, neither could remember each other. However, we immediately laughed hysterically because we did acknowledge that we were not straight A students. If we were, we would have recognized one another! Since then, every single time we meet, the personal but casual conversation seem to follow a pattern. James will respond with a great sense of humor or deep meaning instantaneously by quoting from ancient Chinese proverbs, poems or folksongs.

One time he and I were trying to remember specifically where we sat in our classroom. In Taiwan, from elementary to high school class, there are about fifty kids in each room. Students are arranged and seated by homeroom teacher based on student's height; the shorter ones are in the front whereas the taller classmates in the back.

Therefore, I asked James where was his seat at our grade school classroom. Instead of answering me, he started to sing this old folksong named *Little Grass,* the theme of the song was far beyond the subject of height. His singing brought my tears. It goes like this:

> *I have no fragrance like the flower, nor am I like a tree.*
> *Rather, I am just little, little one.*
> *No one notices the grass so small.*
> *But I am not lonely! Not at all*
>
> *Look at my companions, stretching from sky to sea!*
>
> *When spring comes, the wind blows me to green.*
> *When the Sun rises, it shines upon me.*
> *Rivers Flowering from the mountains to feed me.*

James and I reconnected thanks to the efforts of Charles, our leader, who thoughtfully created the opportunity for these moments. Recently, James organized a cross country camping trip for some young Chinese friends who visit national parks across America. James wanted his friends to learn about the famous Gateway Arch which symbolized the Gateway to the West.

When they arrived in St Louis, James introduced his camping friends to me. To my surprise, some had traveled from Taiwan just to tour America camping. They all marveled at the magnificent Arch and why and how it was built. While we were at the top windows of the Arch, looking down at the Mississippi River, James pointed to his Chinese camping friends and then to the Arch, he said,

"This is where the East Meets the West!"

After visiting the Arch, as we walked down the hill, James quickly ran toward me and held my arm so I would not fall; I complimented him for being a great Chinese gentleman who respected "elderly" woman since I was the oldest female figure amongst his friends. James grinned and said,

"This is exactly what our old Chinese saying: **Friendship is like wine-the-older the better**." Then pointing to his younger female camping friends, he said,

"Oh, these younger generation have their job too!."

What jobs? I wondered.

"The guys' job is to take turns driving during the daytime. Every night while we are camping, the girls cook homemade Chinese food using just one wok and a two-layer bamboo steamer."

How and why? I was very curious!

"The bottom part of the wok is for cooking soup. The bamboo steamer is placed on top of the wok. One layer is for cooking rice. The other is the mixture of meat and vegetable. Every dinner we have plenty of vegetables with some meat, soup as well as some fresh fruits. It is efficient and healthy."

His explanation brought back our grade school memories. Every morning, before first hour, students gathered on the campus where the PE teacher stood on the platform, leading us in exercise. Then, we sang a song, titled, *The Hygiene 10 Rules*. One of the rules was to eat vegetable, fruits and tofu everyday. These 10 Rules are:

Rule 1. Remember to wash hands thoroughly before and after meals.
Rule 2. Divide your things clearly, never share your tea cup, rice bowl or towel with anyone.
Rule 3. Have vegetables with tofu soup, plus fresh fruits and eggs every day, it will give you health.
Rule 4. Go "number 2", on time, at least once a day.

Rule 5. Stick out your chest, maintain proper posture standing or walking.
Rule 6. Bring your handkerchief and cover your mouth and nose when you cough or sneeze.
Rule 7. Take a bath or shower at least once a day.
Rule 8. Go outside and play at least 2 hours a day.
Rule 9. Always remember to brush your teeth, once in the morning and once at night; make sure to brush between your teeth too.
Rule10. Early to bed for you. Get 10 hours for better energy.

Old memories of those six years of innocent days brought us joy when we all sang (Right) this old song *"The Hygiene 10 Rules"* together at Napa Valley and at the Golden Gate Park during our class reunion of 2015.

This song brought happy tears in our eyes. James still prefers to eat Chinese food daily which consists of more vegetables than meat without dessert. This is something he has done since he came to America 40 years ago. Also, we all noticed that James always walks the stairs and never uses the elevator. No wonder in our reunions, even though not one is seemingly overweight, yet, James is the trimmest one. I realize that these 10 daily rules of hygiene has had positive impact on all of us.

Since retiring from teaching seven years ago, I have reflected on my experiences with my siblings and classmates. We are children of Chinese parents and parents of American-born children. We have fundamental Chinese heritage and have learned the American values of independent, humanity, justice and equality.

All my grade school classmates and I were born in China. When we visit Mainland China, we no longer feel it is our homeland. When we visit Taiwan, we don't feel that is where we belong. Although we have all retired now and lived in the United States for decades, we are still foreigners. I think by the time we leave this world, our generation will be *"Gone with the Wind."*

In my grade school, there were eight classes. Each class was given a name that related to our roots and culture: Loyalty, Filial Piety (or Obedience to your parents), Kindness or Benevolence, Love, Trust, Morality, Harmony, and Balance. My grade school class was the class of **Trust**. We trust our classmates and each other's friendship wholeheartedly.

As Chinese proverb stated:

> *A life without a friend is a life without sun.*

> *Friendship multiplies joys and divides sorrow.*

Our roots are in China, but we have been transplanted in the USA. We have learned to trust our deeply rooted values as we meet new friends in America.

The deeply-rooted values allowed us to develop an appreciation for our new friends Since I have befriended many Americans who have inspired me to fully appreciate American culture through each one's unique spirit - independence, justice, humanity, individuality, creativity. This book: ***Americans The Beautiful*** is my gift to all of my American friends.

Left to right: James Hwang, Steve Ruzicka, Steve Chen, Bess Chen, Theresa Liu and Charles Cha at Ensenada, Mexico in 2015.

A Sea of Love

Wash over Us

海內存知己

天涯若比鄰

American, the beautiful

Anonymous

At the age of 47, he lost his beloved wife.

Listening to his memories of his married life, I felt his deep love for his wife. Their love for each other touched me profoundly. Being the free-spirited person I am, I gave him some free advice,

*"You **loved** your wife! It is a great loss, so it is okay to cry. She is in a happy place now, no longer suffering physical pain, so I am happy for her."*

He may not openly shed tears for the loss of his wife, but I have witnessed how he has shared his love with his family, friends, and even strangers. To me, he is truly a beautiful American.

Seahorse

"If you were an animal, what would it be and why?"

On one occasion, I asked him this question. Before he answered, I quickly gave him mine, *"My first choice would be a seagull. The reason is simple: I love freedom and wish to live by the sea."*

Personally, I think this is an intriguing analogy because the answer reflects what we really want to be and why. This question was first posed to me by a psychology professor during my junior year at college in Taiwan. This question and its implications has stayed with me throughout my life.

"Right now, a seahorse! Because my three children lost their mom, I need to step up for them."

"Why a seahorse?" I heard the word, seahorse, nothing more.

"A male seahorse is equipped with a pouch so he can carry thousands of eggs until they are fully developed. Now, I need to play the dual roles of mother and father for my children."

"How old were they when they lost their mom?"

"It doesn't matter how old you are when you lose your mother. It is a great loss because motherly love is irreplaceable."

His three children ranged from the teens to early twenties when their mother died of breast cancer. Each year he participates in the Making Strides Against Breast Cancer walk. He attended the college graduations and weddings for all three of his children. As he witnessed each of his children receiving the graduation diploma or exchanging wedding vows, he sensed his wife's spirit was proudly with him as well as with all three of his children during the ceremonies.

Big Brother

Deep in his soul, he has always had an instinctive passion about being a loving father. After his youngest child attended an out-of-town college, he spent his spare time by joining the Big Brother program. He used the opportunity to guide a fatherless boy. He would take the boy to fun places like City Museum or outdoor activities such as bike riding or playing basketball or skate boarding in the Forest Park. In addition, he would teach him how to be a responsible student in school and a respectful son to his mother. For example, while playing basketball, he would ask the young boy what he had done to help his mom. He always used the teachable moment.

"Where did you get the idea for joining the Big Brother program?" I was very curious because I had never heard of that type of organization while growing up in Taiwan.

He contemplated for awhile and humbly replied,

"Actually I was involved in the Big Brother program in my early twenties before I married my wife...I guess being raised in a Catholic family with five brothers may have planted the seeds in my soul that I always feel the need to help others."

Giant Chess Set at St. Louis City Museum

The City Museum used to be the International Shoe Company building in St. Louis. In 1997, it was remodeled and repurposed in order to create a large museum that has been an eclectic children's playground, full of tunnels, slides, and other attractions made from architectural and industrial objects. Each time he and his children visited the City Museum, it inspired his creativity. Years later, in his garage, he made a giant chess set. Each piece is 3 and 1/2 feet tall, with a total of 32 pieces. The final touch was painting the chess set with the colors blue and yellow symbolizing the St. Louis Rams football team. He presented his donation, a giant chess set, to the City Museum. The manager was delighted. It was 2001, five years after his wife had passed away.

When I asked him why the City Museum and why the chess set? His reply was,

"City Museum is a fun place for the kids...no age limit... kids can have a wild fun time with their parents...I taught my kids to play chess while they were growing up... Now, when they come home any time, we play checkers or chess; we always have family fun time together...There is no age limit for fun!"

<u>Fast forward</u>: He is a man of great dedication and patience. I saw this when he applied himself every afternoon in his workshop to reconstruct, sand, and repaint the giant chess set that he made in 2001. In 2016, each day after his grandsons came home from school, they would work together to rebuild the whole set.

After the project was completed, the grandsons helped load the thirty-two pieces of giant chess set on the truck and went to the city.

When I asked him why he wanted his two teenaged grandsons to come along with him, his answer was,

"Nothing is ever easy, even a good deed; it would be a good idea if the boys learned how to donate their time and effort for the good of the community."

On the arrival, two grandsons helped their grandpa with delivering the giant chess set pieces, one by one to the City Museum. The director gratefully accepted his donation once more.

After the chess set was delivered, grandpa paused. While contemplating the day's events, a warm smile appeared on his face, and he recalled:

"...hmmm... a special meaning about the giant chess set... there was a giant chess set inside the main hall at Pere Marquette State Park where my honeymoon was ... my wife and I had such fun playing the giant chess set there..."

There is something to be said for legacy. Just think of the example this grandpa is setting for his grandsons!

Grandpa's Journal

In my opinion, he is the greatest grandpa in the world.

He has made a conscious decision and effort to spend as much time as possible with his grandchildren, focusing on the activities that they enjoy.

Each of his two grandsons has their own interest. He goes fishing with one grandson who loves fishing in a kayak. He buys baseball season tickets for the other one so they could see Cardinal ball games together. Grandpa goes bike riding with both grandsons.

He keeps two separate journals about his time with each grandson. Sometimes, next to his light-hearted writing, there is an attachment with pictures he has taken. Each grandson is encouraged to jot down a few words in his own journal, too.

Grandpa's notes: *...played indoor basketball against the boys; they won 8 to 7; ...right before I left, helped boys with home work; ...helped the boys play a card game against their mom and me; ...for the first time! Way to go! (picture with his grandson riding his bike);... played in the creek, great day! (picture in the woods);... You are a great kid!... you are one of America's greatest kids!...you out fished me!; ...thanks for a fun day! ... Father's Day, we sat on the back porch and took turns reading "To Kill a Mockingbird";...Thank you so much for coming over for three hours and helping me to shovel snow;...You are so busy playing in the marching band, playing on the baseball team, cutting grass and being very responsible...I am so proud of you...!*

Five Fishing Poles

Fishing is one of his hobbies. While he frequently brings his fisherman grandson, every few months he will go off on his own to fish. Yet, when he does it, he always purchases five fishing poles first and some worms at Walmart. Then, he heads for his destination. Once he is there, he walks to his own spot where he places his chair facing the pond down the hill. Next, he lays each pole by the pond; five of them in a row. Then, he casts the lines out into the pond, waiting to catch his fish and his fishing "buddies". Within an hour, there are kids ranging in age from

5 to 15 who come around followed by their parents or older brothers. These are his new fishing buddies. He always waves at them first, then asks the same question,

"Would you like to learn how to fish?"

All the kids are excited to learn! He patiently shows them one by one how to hook the worm, and how to cast the line. Needless to say, the last stage of fishing is instinctive as they start to sense when to pull. He loves to see the kids' excitement when they catch a fish from the pond. He always encourages kids to take the fishing pole home with their trophies.

The last time was a "first." He took his grandson along to this special park without mentioning where or giving any specific reason. He explained this reason:

"This time I just told him that we were going to a special park without a kayak. I wanted him to be around with other kids without noticing differences. Kids are just kids."

"And?" I looked at him and asked, *"Did he catch any fish?"*

"He had so much fun that it didn't matter whether or not he caught any fish himself because he was so busy teaching and helping other kids learn how to fish!"

Suddenly, *one of Confucius sayings came to me:*
* **Give me a fish and I eat for a day. Teach me to fish and I eat for a lifetime.**

Christmas Gifts

Every Christmas Eve, he takes a stack of $50 bills and drives to the city where charity organizations sell inexpensive used items. His early morning arrival on that day has only one purpose. He seeks a parent with a child...a mother or grandmother who impresses him with their care and nurturing.

After carrying on a brief casual conversation with her, he then places one of the $50 bills into the mother's hand and leaves the place in no time. When I heard about his personal charitable action from a reliable source, I begged him to bring me along and watch him "in action." I promised him I would not reveal his identity. Once he agreed, I asked him my very first question:

"Why on the morning of Christmas Eve?"

"If a mother buys Christmas gifts on the very last day at a shopping place like that, you know they are needy and desperate to find something for the little ones in their care."

That day I followed him to Goodwill. It took only a short period of time walking around inside the Goodwill. I saw him talking with a woman who stood in front of a large toy which was a plastic kitchen oven, she touched and touched; she looked and looked, totally focusing on this over-sized toy for a long while. Then, I heard him asking,

"Isn't this oven fun to have? Are you buying this for your daughter?"

"Oh yeah, for my granddaughters. They all would love this!"

"How many granddaughters do you have? "

"I have twelve grandkids, five granddaughters..., this oven got everything! Mmm... they would love this big oven...But...but... its $12.00!"

He walked closer to her and extended his hand with $50.00 cash in it. While shaking hands with her, I heard him say,

"Merry Xmas! This is for your granddaughters." He turned around and immediately walked away.

The woman's jaw just dropped and her eyes popped when she found the $50.00 cash mysteriously in her hand. She literally screamed and shouted,

"Praise the Lord! Praise the Lord! " She realized what was happening and looked for the "Santa Claus." But, by that time, her Santa had already disappeared. Her eyes filled with joyful tears. Mine, too.

Coffee Break

Some of my friends and I like to meet up at a coffee house frequented by Washington University students. The atmosphere of the coffee house reminds me of the Tea House near National Taiwan University during my college days. Back then, the Tea House was our "intellectual social media" where college students exchanged study tips and other academic information. That day, several Washington U students apparently were doing their homework there. I love this coffee house even more!

On one late morning, while my friends were waiting for the food we all ordered at this coffee house, he "disappeared". A few minutes later, I looked outside noticing that he was sitting on the street corner by the curb talking to a young man. It appeared he was talking to his friend's son. Few minutes later, the waiter brought us our sandwiches then walked outside to give the last one to the young man on the street.

"Did you treat your friend's son to a special lunch today?" I asked.

"No, I don't know him... he is a homeless."

"Wow! You just gave a homeless person lunch? Today is his lucky day! " I commented.

"Well! After listening to his personal tragedy, I asked how he was going to turn his life around. That church offers temporary jobs from time to time to the homeless people if they choose to work..." He stopped and

pointed to the building across the street from the coffee house. Then he continued, *" So, he goes there everyday to try. But, no job today, no money, no food today, so I bought him a hamburger today for not giving up on trying to find a job."* After listening to what he did for this homeless man, it touched my heart. One of Confucius sayings silently springs to mind.

* **Better to light a candle than to curse the darkness.**
* **When the winds of change blow, some people build walls and others build windmills.**

Everyday With Mom

When his mother was in the final stages of her life, he visited her daily. With a big smile on his face and looking at his mother, he sat at her bedside and held his mother's hand while patiently listening to the words of wisdom from his mother's inaudible voice. Then he got an idea from one of his favorite books, **_tuesdays with Morrie_**. He went out and bought a notebook and wrote _Everyday with Mom_ on the front page. The notebook was placed on the table right next to the chair in his mother's bedroom. He invited his seven siblings and visitors to write down their fond memories or thoughts about their mom during each visit.

His mother was a very wise woman who had a positive influence on her son. She was calm and peaceful each time when I paid my visit. Then one day, being the only visitor, I couldn't hide my curiosity. I asked her the key to her tranquility and how she equalized her motherhood among eight adult children. She smiled and said,

"Everyone has their own issue. I listen with all my heart. After they leave, I close the closet (her term for a special place for each personal issue) *with my own prayer for each one."*

For his mom, each and every person was honored. Like mother, like son!

Sunset over the Rainbow

He has this an unconditional compassion for senior citizens. It began one day while he was shopping at the store and noticed a hunched-back, old lady using a walker. He observed how difficult the task was for her and he realized that she could not reach an item on the shelf.

"Ma'am, may I help you?"

"Yes." She pointed to a door handle. He reached out and gave it to her, then he politely asked,

"Do you need any help to install it? I would be glad to help you."

The next day, after her door handle was installed in the bathroom, he told her whenever she needed help to just gave him a call. Since then, he has done many things for her; he has been there for her when she fell down in the garage; he removed the large fallen tree branches on the driveway after the storm; he drove her to her relative's funeral service in another city two hours away; he took her to visit her 85 year-old sister in the nursing home; he responded to her request to help her elderly neighbor with building a birdhouse so her neighbor could watch birds and wouldn't feel lonely.

"Where did you get this incredible passion for helping the elderly people?" I asked.

"I got it when my grandpa was very old and couldn't get out of bed. At the time, I was about 8 or 9 years old. He needed me there and was always so happy to see me. Those elderly citizens remind me of my grandpa."

"Do you feel sorry for them because they are at the end of their journey?"

He was somewhat in shock that I made that statement, I knew I was not being politically correct, due to my own natural aging process. His response surprised me, and yet it was totally understandable. His reply is the reflection of how his grandpa blessed him.

*"Actually, **I am the lucky one that I get to help them.** When I see their smiles, it reminds me of the sunset over the rainbow!"* In my heart, I couldn't help but singing:
> ***Somewhere Over the Rainbow! What a Wonderful World!***

      ************   *********   **********

I have always been impressed with the generous attitude of so many Americans. It is a quality that brings meaning to the song, **"America The Beautiful."** This is just one special story.

North to Alaska

Brother Joe

Brother Joe is the first and only person I know who lives in Alaska. He chose to live there 25 years ago.

Before I met him, I knew very little about Alaska. It is a state located way up north -- "North to Alaska." Yep! Back in the 60s, while the movie *North to Alaska* was showing at the theater, the theme song by Johnny Horton was played on the radio in Taipei, Taiwan. Each time my five high school best friends and I heard that music, we would sing along whole-heartedly without knowing the depth of the meaning of the lyrics. But we could sure sing every word of the song loud and clear, even with a touch of American country twang. Today, I still remember part of the lyrics.

Way up north, North to Alaska...

They crossed the Yukon River and they found the bonanza gold.
Below that old white mountain just a little south-east of Nome
Sam Crossed the Majestic mountains to the valleys far below

He talked to the team of huskies as he mushed on through the snow...
'Cos a man needs a woman to love him all the
time...a true love is hard to find.
I'd build for my Ginnie, honeymoon home.

Where the river is winding, big nuggets they're finding.
North to Alaska, go north, the rush is on

Brother Joe! Not Father Joe?

"I am a Franciscan brother, not a priest." Joe said. *"It was my choice not to be priest."*

I hadn't realized until then that entrants had to make a conscious choice between brother and priest before entering the priesthood. Why did Joe choose to become a brother and not a priest? I wondered.

"While I was growing up, the very first thing I wanted to do was to be a fireman or policeman, or something in service-related work...I grew up in a Catholic family and I remember Father Myron the most during my St. Anthony Elementary School and St. Joseph Franciscan Seminary High School years. He was like a father to me...down to earth...took us to the zoo...to different places....

... Actually he was not a priest, he was a brother. He would always work in the kitchen, garden, did maintenance kinds of jobs. He did not tell people, 'This is a sin or not a sin' thing...he just worked with people. I was influenced by his humanity and his kindness while growing up. After one year at Quincy College in Illinois, I decided to pursue the priesthood by attending St. Joseph's Seminary for Franciscan priests."

I couldn't help but interrupt him. *"Did your parents approve of your decision?"*

In Taiwan, my parents would tell us whom we should date, marry, or which career we should pursue. Based on the scores of our individual college entrance exams, The Department of City Education would decide which college we would attend and what major we would study. I wondered if a young Chinese son decided to become a Buddhist monk after finishing his freshman year in college, what would his parents say?

14

Brother Joe's experience sounds like a typical American one.

*"Mom and Dad were happy with my decision to become a Franciscan priest. However, later, when I decided to be a brother instead of a priest, they were a bit concerned. It was because the priest is 'high up' there, whereas the brother is way down low. Then, after I told my parents that I didn't want to say Mass, I didn't need to be the boss, didn't like to tell people how to live their lives...it's just not me...I liked to be the person who lived with people, worked with the poor ... **As brother, I can allow people to be who they are and I can live with people whatever condition they are in.** After listening to my reasoning and motivation, my parents said that if I was happy with my decision, they would be happy too..."*

How much training did he need?

*"It took three years of intensive training in Westmont, Illinois. I can still remember as I was preparing for my final vows of **chastity, obedience, and poverty.** One of the Franciscan priests said to me, 'This is for life.' ...*

...One of the brothers later told me that I looked really, really sick before the ceremony started... I looked like something else was really bothering me... But, afterwards, I looked so happy!...

What happened?

...On that final vow day, I knew I really had to take my vows seriously. I knew I had time to change my mind, to rethink it all the way up to the time when I made my definitive decision by saying these words...

*...'**I will be a Franciscan, I will live poorly, I will be chaste, I will be obedient to my brothers.'***

... Once I made those promises, I knew I would be making those promises for life...

Chastity

...I had a close girlfriend before that point. And, this was an important decision too...In my heart, it was clear that I heard my mind saying, 'I truly choose this life, I want to be a Franciscan brother...I have to choose between these two: God and the girl! I chose God, so I have to be faithful to God...' I still remember telling her that, my ultimate goal is to serve God...I have not seen her for 30 years...

Obedience

... One of the Franciscan brothers asked me if I wanted to attend cooking school to learn to be a chef. I said, 'Really?' The brother said, 'We want you to try it!' The next thing I knew, I was taking two years of cooking class at culinary art school in Chicago, because this was what they wanted me to do... I had always wanted to work in poor areas where people did not have anything. Next thing I knew, I was assigned to Cleveland where I was cooking for parishioners and brothers who wanted to be priests. I stayed in Cleveland for ten years...

Unexpectedly, Brother Joe stopped and grinned.

...There is a cute story during my time in Cleveland. One night, a guy came, we just finished eating everything. He asked me if it was okay to eat something, I said, 'Yeah, yeah.' I went to the kitchen and brought him a plate of spaghetti. He said, 'Oh! This is my favorite food!' Then he gave me a dollar...

...Next day, he came back and asked me, 'Can I borrow a dollar?' This went on four or five times with one dollar going back and forth. Usually people came and were given a sandwich, they ate, and left. But, for him, each time he came, I got the chance to spend time talking with him. To him, showing his gratitude by giving me a dollar, even if it was not much, was his way of appreciating what I did. Not long after that, he died...

... During that time, I worked in the neighborhood teaching the Bible to families, just reading and talking about what we read and applying it to our lives. It was in a poor area. Then, I was told I should think about working in another poor area. Meanwhile, one of the bishops invited us to go to Alaska." Brother Joe paused; smiled and said,

"I realized everything that had happened was to prepare me for the road to Alaska."

Poverty

"When I volunteered to move to Alaska, I was given a six-page document *describing what to expect: mosquitoes, alcoholic drinking, isolation, suicide, few roads, plane travel to reach villages... It gave me pause and concern. I told three other brothers that I was the wrong guy, but they said 'It's okay.' So I went. But after just one week there in Alaska, I told those brothers, 'You know what? I am going to be here for twenty years.' I felt right at home!"*

Hunt for Moose!

"I was with two Notre Dame sisters when I killed my first moose. During that day, they taught me how to survive, how to hunt, and how to roast...

... We worked two hours straight on this huge animal skinning the meat. In my cooking class, I had learned how to cut meat, so I knew where to find the joint...but, this was my first time cutting a giant animal! ...

...Then I looked at the two sisters and asked 'What do we do now?' Both sisters answered, 'We don't know.' By that time, I realized I was the one who would have to deal with this huge animal: cut it, pack it up, and get it back... I was so busy working that giant animal, although it was 20 below zero, I didn't feel cold. When it was done, my hair was snow white... While we were trying to get out of there, we got stuck in the snow with a thousand pounds of moose meat...

... I said to the two sisters, 'You know what? We didn't pray and thank God for the food.' So, we stopped and prayed, and we also prayed for the help to get back. Sure enough, the snow machine started working and we returned to safety!"

Fishing for King Salmon

"Salmon is the main fish in Alaska. I learned how to catch these thirty-five-pound fish using a net about 100 feet long. After catching these big salmon, I asked how they could be preserved for the winter. First, I was told that we cut them into half-an-inch strips, then dip them in the salt water, and finally hang them to dry like jerky or smoke them. After three days, put them in jars. Sometimes, we add some hot chili peppers or garlic...

Planting Vegetables

... In the summer time, we grow our own vegetables in the garden like turnips, giant cabbage, potatoes, and sweet potatoes. Then, we begin the canning process."

Brother Joe not only hunts and fishes with native Alaskans, but he also plants vegetables and shares them. It made me wonder about his role there? Spiritual leader? So, I asked;

"Are you spreading Catholicism?" Surprisingly, he gave me a decisive answer:

"Oh no! The native Alaskan Indians have their own strong sense of God!"

Sense of God

"I am here not for the lifestyle...not because I want to be a hunter for sport, or a fisherman.. I am here because of the people of Alaska...There have been priests and sisters in this area to keep the faith going. Alaskan Indians have their own real strong sense of God...

...They like the ravens...To them, the raven is 'the' spiritual animal; it is the animal closest to God because ravens are as unpredictable as nature and its seasons...They are believed to be shape-changers that can assume any form - human or animal, but show pity for the people...

...Many Native Alaskans believe that the ravens are one of the smartest animals because they can imitate human speech or be extremely playful. They can make very sophisticated non-vocal signals; they are adaptable and show empathy for each other...

...For Alaskan Indians, the raven has a unique spirit and is one of the most intelligent birds. A raven does not discriminate between humans and animals. Because of their fascinating skills, they rescue beings from floods, save human lives...they are found everywhere in Alaska from deserts to mountains -- a feat requiring exceptional intelligence..."

Brother Joe went on to explain how Alaskan beliefs extend to practical situations.

"One time, because of a snow machine accident, two men were drowned in the river and their bodies were not found. One of the native Alaskan Indian elders said to me that by following their tradition of building a fire, burning food, and saying a prayer, the river would release the dead bodies...So I led the prayer... Half-hour later, one body showed up."

American Catholic vs. Alaskan Indian

To me, Brother Joe's role is a spiritual leader, I wondered what role his Catholic faith played in his work with the Alaskan people.

***"As God sees it, we all are one together. I am here only as an instrument to help the Alaskan Indians and their spirituality. I** have different roles to play, but I am always here to help them; not to judge them."*

Brother Joe understands humanity. We are all human! That caused me to think about the song that I learned to sing in Taiwan. If I were a songwriter or poet, *North to Alaska* would be written for Brother Joe:

Way up north, North to Alaska!
They're goin' North, the rush is on. They crossed the Yukon River
Where the river is winding,
Life's purpose I'm finding.
North to Alaska

A Postscript on Pope Francis

Pope Francis is the 266th and current Pope of the Roman Catholic Church. Brother Joe is the right person to ease my deep rooted inquisitive mind about what his personal view about the Holy Man. He said;

*"I am impressed and touched when Pope Francis told thousands of journalists that he took to heart the words of his best friend Claudio Hummes' advice - **Don't forget the poor!**"...Personally, I like what he believes and his actions...his belief is that **the church and spirituality need to be rebuilt again, not just the buildings, but the people...** Pope Francis' compassion starts with his non-judgmental approach... Christ never judged, gay or not, mothers who are married or not. Pope Francis **encourages all the religions to come together in the spirit of Christ**...the important things are we shouldn't fight over the spirit of Christ, or God."*

Pope Francis lives by example. Brother Joe lives by example, too!. My feeling is that wherever Brother Joe is, God is there.

American Dad, China Hope

Dave Murphy

One Saturday morning, I watched Dave and his middle-school daughter, Lily, walk toward my front door; they were coming so that I could tutor Lily in math, yet I got the feeling that the visit could turn out to be about much more.

On the table, Lily laid out all the materials I asked her to bring: math textbook, recent notes, and quizzes that would help me decide how much time each week we would need to meet.

After looking over her notes, I thumbed through her tests and quizzes and saw that her lowest score was a 92. What? Why are they here? Lily obviously didn't need help with.

"*You are in middle school, but what grade?* " I asked, thinking that the quadratic formula, which I saw in her papers, was usually taught in 9th grade algebra.

"*8th grade,*" Lily answered softly.

"*Are you in the regular math class?*"

"*Um...*" She shyly gave me an unfinished answer, so her father, Dave, replied,

"*She is in the 8th grade honors math class.*"

Dave's answer was a total surprise to me. I used to teach high school students with math and didn't realize that an honors math class existed or was even needed in middle school.

"What do you want my help with?" I asked Lily. She gave me a small smile. Dave stepped in to help his daughter by answering the question, almost apologetically.

"She wants to improve her grade from A- to A+ in her math class."

I was speechless. Later that day I told my daughter, Helen, about Lily's request. Helen proclaimed that Lily has genuine Chinese DNA because she was born in China. Even though Helen's father and I were both born in China, yet Helen was born in Texas. She feels that this is the reason why math was not her best subject -- a genetic 'Texan' mutation that affected her true Chinese math abilities.

I was struggling to understand what was motivating Lily to be the best of the best. If her goal was to get A+ in honors math, what about her other subjects? Dave said,

"She is also in honors science and English classes."

It was obvious that Lily didn't need any extra help from me. I decided to approach this differently. I asked to speak with Lily alone.

"What do YOU want to be when you grow up to be an adult woman?" The 14-year-old Chinese girl gave me an immediate answer.

"Obstetrician."

"Why?"

"To help to bring babies to the world."

Lily answered me with 100 percent confidence. Her shyness disappeared, and there was no doubt in my mind that her decision was clearly defined. So was my prediction about her future -- a conscientious and successful physician.

Silently I prayed that her biological mother in China knew that her daughter was doing exceptionally well in America. If there were magic powers that I could use to communicate with her birth mother, I would tell her that her daughter's success in school and her determination towards her future was shaped and nurtured by her very loving American dad – Dave Murphy.

A Baby's Journey from China to America

Through suggestions and arrangements from the adoption agency, *China Hope,* all the American soon-to-be parents flew to Beijing, the capital of China. They stayed in the same hotel for several days. During that time, it was recommended that they would visit some of the city's great tourist sites -- The Great Wall, Tiananmen Square, the Forbidden City, and more.

Some parents, like Dave, made their own itinerary.

"Because of government activities going on in Tiananmen Square, we went with other couples to see some less famous temples and markets along the Silk Road. It was very exciting to see these famous historical places in Beijing, one of the world's greatest cities. But in our own hearts, we couldn't wait to see our first child, our first daughter. Visiting Beijing was secondary."

At that time, their adopted daughter, Lily, was physically at the other side of China. But Lily has their hearts every second while they were in Beijing. When they were back at the hotel after touring the city in those few days, they took out their only picture of their soon-to-be daughter every chance they could and looked at her over and over again.

She looked much smaller than her age of 14 months old. The picture was as small as a postage stamp. It was their only possession from her,

23

other than two pages of simple medical records, in which some babies' birth days were projected by the orphanage. The birth parents dropped the babies off in various public places without any written notes. Therefore, the orphanage had to guess at the approximate birthday. Dave's daughter was found at the police station by the Yangtze River. Luckily, her birth mother left a note indicating her birthday.

After touring Beijing for several days, they flew to the city of Chongqing of Sichuan province in southwestern China. Five couples and two single women, all soon-to-be American parents, were staying in the same hotel.

On their first day, they reported to the director of Social Welfare Home/Orphanage. After paying an adoption fee, they were invited to look around the orphanage.

These 12 anxious American parents looked through a window across the balcony and tried to guess which seven babies belonged to them. Later that afternoon, the parents were advised to purchase baby formula and other food for travel back to United States. Each couple was given a list of items to shop for at the recommended nearby store owned by the local government, called "Friendship."

The second day was D-day -- Delivery Day. "The Moment" arrived when the parents were told by orphanage officials to "Get ready!" Instantly, the parents scrambled to get preparations ready in the hotel room. The director took them to the orphanage for the ceremony. After the parents paid their second adoption fee to the bookkeeper, the caretakers brought in the babies.

As Dave reminisced about that day and his anticipation at seeing his daughter for the first time, I was reminded of when I first saw my own daughter, Helen. Just like any first-time mom, I will always remember *the exciting touching moment.* My daughter Helen was brought in by the nurse in the hospital in Lubbock, Texas to my bedside.

I wondered about the similarities of that special experience for adoptive parents.

"Talking about that moment brings back nice memories. I remember when I first laid my eyes on her...

Dave was getting emotional.

... It was a cold and damp March day and the children were layered with clothes. A supervisor of the caretakers would announce the parents' name, like 'Baby for Smith' or 'Baby for Murphy,' and parents would go up to get their daughters...

...Each had a short note about the baby's personality -- I think each note was about the same, like 'Happy Baby' or 'Baby Formula' or 'Sweet Candy' ...When I first saw Lily, she was wrapped in so many layers; her hair was all sweaty and wet from perspiration. She was smiling. It seemed like she was a bit confused about all the activity and attention, but I held her and spoke to her in soft tones...

... Later, when Lily was brought back to the hotel room, the first thing we did was get her bathed and into warm new clothes. Just like a Russian doll, we peeled back layer after layer of clothes. 'Where is the kid?' Finally, after four or five layers, split pants, and a diaper that looked pretty worn out, there she was ready for her bath. She was giggling during the whole process, as if to say, 'Ha-ha...you cannot find me yet...I am playing hide-and-seek inside these clothes.' Dave stopped and said,

*"For me, life really changed in those first few moments. Suddenly, things had a few level of importance and meaning. No longer was it enough to get by and live for the next event. Now, there was a new sense of purpose : To **guide, to coach, to care, to support, to demonstrate principles."***

His experience touched my heart; I wanted to hear more from him about that special night, an American man who just became a Chinese girl's father.

"In the middle of the first night, I held her in my arms and walked around the hotel room. When I giggled at her, at that moment, I realized I was holding a human being, one on one. I giggled at her more, and she

responded more. We were connecting as a father and daughter. At that precise moment, I wanted to have another baby."

Those moments were echoed and fortified when Jess, their second adopted daughter from southern China, in the city of Yangjing of Guangdong province, came into their lives in 2004.

Dave is now raising two teenage daughters. Each with totally different personalities, and yet they each complement each other. Each girl has her own musical talent. Lily plays violin, and Jess plays guitar. The American dad described his daughters' different characters to me.

"Lily is a natural born leader who is very self-motivated and an action taker. For example, when we first adopted Lily in China, even though she was 14 months old, she could not walk. After we came back to America, the day care center found her condition somewhat peculiar. They told us to give her one more week, and if she still could not walk, then she might have a genetic physical impairment...

... She surprised all of us by standing up straight and walking within a week. Our conclusion was that she was in the crib all day long since the day she was placed at the orphanage. She might not have had many opportunities to be held or encouraged to walk until the day we came to adopt her. I think it tells me that she is intelligent and has a strong motivation to succeed."

What about Jess?

"It took us about a year and half to go through the adoption procedure for Lily, but much less time for Jess because the orphanage at her birth place got shut down due to flu in the Guangdong Province where Jess was found...

...Jess is witty, observant and funny; she is a commentator and an artist." David smiled and gave me an example about Jess.

"Let me give you one story to show Jess's natural theatrical performance ability. On a Saturday morning at a Parkway School Musical Recital, as I was watching Jess playing guitar on the stage, she kept looking at the

other guitar players. I thought she looked somewhat shy. After the recital was over, I asked her whether she was nervous on stage, but her answer was 'no!' Then I asked why not? She said, 'It is not about me! We are there to interpret the music.' She was only 8 years old."

While listening to Dave's candid conversation about his two adoring Chinese daughters, I tried to put myself in his shoes and wondered how people perceive him as an American dad with Chinese daughters.

"I don't pay attention to what people think or say. Lily and Jess are my daughters; I never see them as my Chinese daughters. Just like any other father, I do things with my daughters like shopping, taking them to music lessons, dance practice, gym and ice-skating. We take winter trips to the south, and in summer, we visit my hometown of Boston, where they get to see my family."

Boston Strong

Dave was raised in an environment where intellect, culture, and history were strong influences. In college, he majored in Government and minored in Psychology. After he graduated from a private college in Connecticut, he frequently spent time listening to lectures or speeches from famous political figures like Colin Powell at Harvard night school.

It was natural for Dave to be tuned in to how the government works and how its policy affects people. His own family members live in the Wellesley area. His father was a history teacher and his brother is a lawyer. Ivy League colleges like MIT, Harvard, and Wellesley produce successful professionals such as doctors, attorneys, politicians, professors, artists, and engineers. But, Dave holds his own philosophical thoughts about the culture of Boston.

"Growing up in that area was a nice experience to learn about life with people who just happened to be successful parents. A friend's father was the Nobel Prize winning Dr. Murray who was the first surgeon to successfully transplant an organ. But, to me, their kids were just friends or

fellow students. It helped teach me that people are just people. Growing up in Boston gave me a background in diversity. My two daughters were born in China and have now been raised in Midwest America. As their father, I like them to be around people with different ethnic or cultural backgrounds. I like them to be around Chinese in America."

Dave paused, looked at me, and smiled. I finally understood the meaning behind this father-daughter meeting. I felt honored. Dave nodded and continued;

*"I want my two daughters **to explore the world, to learn from mistakes, to ask questions and be flexible enough to know which goals are the really important ones in life**. Most importantly, I want them to **always know that their parents love them.** This is how I grew up and learn these lessons from my parents."*

Listening to Dave's fatherly guidance, one of the Confucius quotes sayings came to me,
* ***Giving your son advice is better than giving him one thousand pieces of gold.***

Celebrating These Special Girls

Twice a year, the adoptive parents in St. Louis reunite with each other by bringing their daughters together. The first is on Chinese New Year's Day, and the other they call, *"Gotchu Day"* to celebrate the day they met each special daughter for the first time in Chongqing.

That year, Dave invited me to his house on Chinese New Year's Day. Looking at the loving American parents doting on their Chinese daughters, I was so moved and could only utter two simple words to each parent from the bottom of my heart, *"Thank you!"*

We, Chinese always use this popular proverb when we meet people unexpectedly and a friendship that was meant to be blossoms:
* ***Fate brings people together no matter how far apart they may be.***

Coming to America - Land Opportunity

Stephen Novack

Growing up in Taiwan, we lived with a constant, subconscious fear before coming to America. There was always some hostility and disapproval from the Communist China government. We were independent but always feared that the Communists would attack and invade Taiwan. We worried about bombs...battles...and war.

Our dream was to escape the fear and stress. America was the land of opportunity and security.

My father wanted all of that and more for us. With his last breath, he whispered to me,

"Study in America! Next century belongs to America." I was 13 years old then.

For my family, political security was important...but we also wanted to be in a place where your intelligence and work would be rewarded. So, after my father passed away, I studied hard all the way through college. In my senior year, like all college students, we focused on preparing to come to America. Boys would serve one year in the military after finishing college. We all had to meet the three major requirements for permission to leave Taiwan for coming to America:

(1) acquiring American graduate school admission;
(2) passing English Proficiency Test;
(3) obtaining legal documentation from
>   a) community health center to prove we were immune from tuberculosis,
>   b) two years living expenses in a bank statement so we wouldn't be financial burden to America, and last,
>   c) statement of no criminal record from the police station.

After coming to the United States, because of higher educational degree we all earned, locating a professional job appeared to be easy and it seemed to me that American employers were all willing to help us in applying for a Green Card to legally live in America. Then we would apply for American citizenship after having 5 years of the green card. That was in the 60's and 70's.

In 2010's, some people came to America from other countries for slightly different reasons, but they followed procedures similar to ours. However, given the danger in their own countries, some immigrants needed even more assistance.

Stephen Novack is an American corporate lawyer specializing in real estate. While his primary practice of law is constant and reliable, he also has expanded his skills to help others who desire stability and reliability.

Volunteer for refugees

"I volunteer my time and skills to help refugees reach their dream and find safer, more productive lives here in America. I started about several years ago volunteering for a non-profit organization. This has become a mutually beneficial situation...I learn more about immigration law...and refugees start new lives."

Who are the refugees?

"I work with lots of refugees from war zones and areas of great disturbance. Afghanistan, Iraq... all of the refugees come here with horrific stories from their homelands...

...Places like Somalia are especially disturbing. There is no effective government. Warrior groups are still attacking each other. These are completely displaced people. Refugee camps offer only temporary and porous protection...

...It is a long process for them to get to the United States. First of all, they have to be accepted into the refugee camp where there are hundreds of thousands of them. There are agreements with the United Nations (UN) to select, interview and transfer only some of those refugees to a new country. The United States is selected for maybe fifty thousands refugees per year from Africa. When they get to the United States, the UN and US government make the arrangements and decisions where they initially go. Of course, they would go where their families are located."

International Institute

"St. Louis is one of the better settlement agencies of the International Institute. The International Institute tries to help refugees through the legal process as well as try to find them suitable employment...

...Refugees get government support for their first two years. This includes assistance in the form of food stamps, housing, medication, and programs to learn English. Once those two years are finished, the people are on their own...

...Then, after five years with a Green Card, they can apply for citizenship."

Oh, yes, it was all familiar to me!

When I applied for American citizenship in early 70's, I had to pass the American Constitution test in the court house, followed by a judge interview in Atlanta, Georgia. I remembered the judge asked me to list 3 of 5 Freedom Rights.

The Judge appeared to be pleased with my simple answer; then nodded, and signed the paper. It was the moment I would never forget when I became an officially legalized American citizen. Stephen continued;

"Refugees need to pass the English and American History tests. Many of them have difficulty learning English so they may not be able to get citizenship. But, they can get a Green card so they can stay in the US...

...Most of my work relates to processing marriages. Though, there are some cases related to breaking the law in the US. In my role, I communicate the laws to the refugees and make sure they understand the impact of any legal issues"

Stephen paused and seemingly he went into deep thought. Then he mentioned two words : Marital Abuse. He explained;

Marital Abuse

"In the last 20 years in the United States, we passed a lot of laws about marital abuse; government cracks down on those abuses, so the effect is tremendous. These are felonies and are treated very seriously by our courts...

...For our clients, these laws can be uniquely problematic. These marital abuse laws are deportable offenses. Spousal abuse is not to be taken lightly and should be prosecuted. However, in the cases of refugees, we have seen incidences of an argument may be communicated as a physical abuse criminal act due to the language gaps. True abuse is never acceptable...

...I help people prepare for their hearings with local immigration officers, allegation hearings, and any other specific issues they may have to contend with on their paths to citizenship. In some cases, I have seen the

results of their horrific lives in their homelands. I have seen fathers injured or maimed from battles. Some have crutches for walking and may not be able to find work easily. Often times, I will take them to the store to get groceries in addition to work on their legal activities."

Wondering what Stephen's personal view was about immigrant's law became my immediate question since I myself was a legalized immigrant.

*"Well, I think America is a big country, there is tremendous resources for this country. Those immigrants have managed to get here, I can't never say that is it, and send them back. You look at the history, **our parents or grandparents were from other countries for chances to have better living, to a land of opportunity..."***

Stephen got up and went to his office and brought out a small statue of Mother Teresa.

Mother Teresa

"This is an example of how difficult is it to work in the legal system and how expensive it is for lawyer to work in that system. You need it, but who has the money for it? ...

...One time, an 18 year old man came to the International Institute with a problem. His issue was that he was recorded as not having registered to be drafted. That is one of the criteria for American citizenship...

...Earlier, he had been asked by his Immigration officer if he had registered for the draft. The language gap resulted in him not understanding the question. The officer recorded a "no" in that space...

...I knew the process and his uneasiness with the language. It was obvious that he did not understand all the steps nor the question. I arranged a follow-up session with the officer and accompanied the man. The record was corrected and, ultimately, he received citizenship."

Stephen stopped and continued,

"Six months later, he went back to visit his country – Albania – as an American citizen. He had left due to unrest...but now he came back with the security of American citizenship. He went back to his country and got engaged. When he came back to St. Louis, he gave me this little Mother Teresa statue."

Why Mother Teresa? This young Albanian man said to Stephen,

"Mother Teresa is from Albania, she is one of the most important people in Albania. Mother Teresa helped me, now you helped me. So I gave you this..."

The reasons of my generation coming for American were for higher education and obtaining American citizenships. Now, we have lived in a land of opportunity for several decades with peace and have learned the respect for the ordinary American citizens who live for the true meaning of democracy.

Listening to Stephen's motivation to help others, Mother Teresa's sayings came to my heart:
*   *If you can't feed a hundred people, then feed just one.*
*   *We feel that what we are doing is just a drop in the ocean. But, the ocean would be less beautiful of that one missing drop.*

Becoming A Doctor, American Way

Jeffrey Marsh

Where does inspiration come from? Before I came to America, I was educated in Taipei, Taiwan in a system that rewards excellence in school with a direction towards advanced careers in medicine, physics or engineering.

Growing up in Taiwan, the entire educational system was very competitive with only those people with the highest grades being afforded the opportunity to advance to the best college.

After I came to America, I met people with wonderful academic backgrounds in successful positions, not only because they had done well in school with high grades, but also because they had a personal passion for their work. Inspiration was from the inside, not just from the teachers and administration.

Dr. Jeffrey Marsh became a doctor, the American way! His story demonstrates the difference between the two cultures. In my culture, occupations were determined by success in school. In America, life experiences along with courses of study help students determine their life's work.

Career Exploration

For most Americans, the path to a career is not straight and direct. There are many side roads and distractions. Like any great exploration, the final destination is made even more glorious and wonderful because of all the views considered along the way.

"When I was a teenager, I was interested in nature and considered becoming a forest ranger. Saving the world was so important to me. Then, I had the opportunity to learn more about the career of a forest ranger. Forest rangers do many great things but they also spend a lot of time sitting in a tower watching for fires. In retrospect, my passion was for ecology, a term unknown to me then... My interest in becoming a forest ranger waned...perhaps there was a better way to save the world..." recalled Dr. Marsh.

Sometimes family knows.

"...My uncle was a doctor in Seattle. During family visits to our home in Los Angeles, he always impressed me. In retrospect, it's hard for me to specify exactly why. Perhaps it was his demeanor, his sense of humanity, his knowledge... But, even before I was able to clearly understand it, the rest of my family had already concluded that I would become a doctor."

What started as an exploration, eventually became his career path. An early advanced educational experience provided an initial opening. In America, some opportunities to try new things are provided. One of those was earned by Dr. Marsh during his junior year of high school - a wonderful, detour from the traditional school advancement path.

"During my junior year in high school, I took an examination, which I passed successfully, to allow me to study at UCLA for half day during my senior year. It provided an incredible opportunity to enter UCLA the following year, upon graduation from High School, as a returning student, not as an incoming freshman. More importantly, I was exposed to classes, students and faculty that had a more advanced view into future careers than a typical teenager may have seen."

Inspiration came from his uncle and the campus of UCLA plus others. His interest was now in medicine.

Johns Hopkins

After studying at UCLA for a period of time, Dr. Marsh focused his aspiration on Johns Hopkins University and the School of Medicine. He was interviewed for the Hopkins accelerated medical program and was accepted. Thus, he received his Baccalaureate degree in 1967 followed by his Medical Doctorate in 1970, both at Hopkins.

Pursuing Specialty

"Once you get into medical school, you rotate through the standard medical specialties: internal medicine, pediatrics, general surgery, and more...

...the idea is to expose you to a variety of disciplines so you may figure out where you belong."

In the U.S., a career path develops from exploration of many ways and approaches and not a set, pre-determined direction.

"In medicine and in life, mentors are incredibly important. During my rotation period, I spent this amazing time with a world-renown hand surgeon. Hand surgery is very delicate and intricate. For example, people like musicians may need meticulous reconstructive surgery. That was my desire to become an exceptional hand surgeon. However, first I had to spend five years becoming trained as a general surgeon before I could be trained as a plastic surgeon and then super specialize after that in hand surgery."

After completing a General Surgery Residency at UCLA, Dr. Marsh moved to Virginia to train in Plastic Surgery with one of the physicians who inspired him during medical school.

"Once I was there, I saw the reality of hand surgery. For the most part, hand surgery is for trauma. This was a night-and-day difference from the surgery for musicians. Most of the patients were laborers with broken bones, dismembered fingers, or worse. The goal of the surgery was to repair. But the patients were not very compliant with therapy or follow up. For me, it was all quite depressing!"

Contemplatively, Dr. Marsh recalled,

"I asked myself: 'Is this what I really want to do?'"

Somewhat depressed, Dr. Marsh reconsidered his path...his direction. Fortune paid a visit in the form of the professor with whom he was training. That surgeon was an expert in reconstructive surgery with specialization in facial birth defects. Consequently, facial reconstructive surgery, especially for children, became his new passion.

"Before finishing my plastic surgery training, I was invited to interview for a job at Washington University School of Medicine in St. Louis. This was very flattering since the Plastic Surgery Division at Barnes Hospital was a preeminent center for plastic surgery training research and creativity through much of the 20th century. I was hired by Washington University to set up a program for surgery for cleft lip/palate and more severe craniofacial defects. I started working there on January 1, 1978. When Washington University decided to build a new Children's Hospital including a surgery suite, I was asked whether I would like to work and have an office at Children Hospital. When I looked at my case load, 80% of my patients were kids. This was not by design. It just happened. So I had unwittingly become a pediatric plastic surgeon and I said, "Sure!"

Listening to his experiences, I was very curious the cause of cleft/lip palate. Dr. Marsh was the first physician that I know of specializing in this reconstructive surgery.

Solving a Puzzle

"The causes of cleft lip/palate include hereditary and environmental factors. Genetics, maternal alcohol abuse, use of some prescription and some recreational drugs, smoking and other activities during pregnancy may contribute to cleft lip/palates...

... As a facial reconstructive surgeon, I see immediate results from the operations I perform. This is immensely gratifying, especially seeing the joy in a parent's face. My personality is not built for the chronic diseases of internal medicine or for the terminal process of dying. Seeing a patient with a cleft lip corrected provides me great satisfaction and pleasure...

... For me, surgery is like solving a puzzle: I analyze the defect, design a solution, and then take the elements apart and put them back together in a more normal way. In many cases, three weeks later my patient is recovered and ready for the future."

Volunteer

I first met Dr. Marsh through his wife, Beki, a foodie like me. He had just come back from Southeast Asia and Thailand where he had attended a medical conference. As my friendship with Beki progressed, I learned that Dr. Marsh went to Thailand and other countries annually. He did volunteer work for the kids with cleft lip/palate by training local surgeons and assisting them in developing interdisciplinary team care with other health professionals such as speech therapists and dentists.

"Sometime in the mid 1980's, I received a phone call from a plastic surgery resident at St. Louis University School of Medicine. He said he was from Thailand originally and was now an American citizen. His intention was to return to Thailand intermittently and provide cleft care for the people there. Interested in advancing his training and experience, he asked if he could observe my work and provide counsel to him..."

A friendship came from this professional experience - a friendship that has opened up more opportunities. But, there was a pause at the beginning.

"… *After not having any contact for ten years, I was surprised when the phone rang and that familiar voice was on the line. He was now practicing in Hawaii…and still going back to Thailand once a year to provide cleft care. He was reaching out to me with a request to go to Thailand and provide my medical teaching services there. No money. No hotel room. No air conditioning…*"

"*Yes! No problem!*" Dr. Marsh responded. He contemplated and said;

"*I savored the opportunity and it was incredibly rewarding. Subsequently I recruited a speech pathologist and a pediatric dentist to accompany me and assist in building a comprehensive cleft care program. My medical trips to Thailand have been illuminating and wonderful!*"

Dr. Marsh has been involved with international medical volunteerism for 23 years. More than just providing medical care, he provided lectures and classroom training, surgical advice, and counsel as well as direction for the creation of clinics. All along the way, he has also explored the culture and the people of Southeast Asia: Bhutan, Cambodia, Laos, and Thailand.

East Meets West

Once a Thai plastic surgery resident asked Dr. Marsh during a drive in Bangkok;

"*Why do you do this? Why do you come here to help train doctors?*"

Dr. Marsh replied;

"*I understand enough of your Thai culture to know that we have different ideas of why things happen. I think I understand that your culture thinks that what happens to you in this life is a function of what you have done in your previous life. So if you were good in your past life, then you should be rewarded, not be punished in this life. But, you don't have control over your life or what is happening...*

...Yet, in my American culture, it is random. It is an accident of birth...of where and who I am. Because of that, I have an incredible opportunity. I came from a family with limited economic means, but I happen to be bright. It was a point of time in America where a lot of resources were invested in education. I was able to get a great education in America and it cost me essentially nothing. And I feel that I have the obligation to pay it back...

*...**I don't pay it back by giving somebody money; I pay it back by helping other people to help other people. I can help by using the tool I got. The tool I have is to teach somebody...**the young plastic surgery resident was quiet a minute; then he said, 'That was really interesting! I have not thought about that' Then I responded by saying, 'Now, you REALLY will think about that!"*

At that moment, two Chinese philosophers' sayings came to my mind:

Confucius:
*   ***The expectations of life depend upon diligence; the mechanic that would perfect his work must first sharpen his tools.***

*   ***To practice five things under all circumstances constitutes perfect virtue; these five are gravity, generosity of soul, sincerity, earnestness, and kindness.***

Lao Tsu - Daoism
*   ***Kindness in words creates confidence. Kindness in thinking creates profoundness. Kindness in giving creates love.***

Jeffrey Marsh is an American doctor, on his path to becoming a philosopher as he reflects on his life's journey. His life experiences and non-traditional route to becoming a doctor took a gratifying and generous turn when he became involved in volunteer services that provided much-needed surgeries for poor people in foreign countries. His willingness to "pay it forward" shows a generosity that goes beyond education.

Postscript:

Following his retirement from full-time surgical practice, Dr. Marsh accompanied by his wife and a small group of long-time healthcare volunteer colleagues continues to do pro bono international cleft lip/palate work in Mexico and Vietnam under the auspices of the International Cleft Care Program of which he is the president.

In 2016, he fulfilled a long deferred goal of becoming certified as a yoga instructor (Yoga Alliance 200) and now is teaching several clients on a one-to-one basis. He and his wife continue to enjoy the Colorado Rockies in all seasons and spending time with their daughter, son-in-law and grandson on the East Coast. Dr. Marsh can only repeat what he's heard from others who retired before him: "How did I ever have time for a full-time job?" There's nothing retiring about his retirement.

Bashert or Destiny

Drs. Lisa & Greg

In Yiddish, "bashert" can best be translated as "what is meant to be." The word is similar to the Chinese word "yu'an" which means a predestined relationship.

Our meeting, and what followed, was "meant to be" for Dr. Lisa, Dr. Greg and me.

What is meant to be does not always follow a logical path. Sometimes the winding and twisting, "destiny" results in wonderful, magical, inspirational moments.

Meant to be

Lisa: My husband and I had a happy married life for 30 years; then he died of bone cancer. One day, my late husband's best friend came to my house and said, 'I know somebody you have to meet. You guys will be perfect for each other. You have to call this guy, his name is Greg.' I said to myself, 'He has to be kidding.' I knew who Greg was. I remembered him from a scientific medical talk he gave to the dermatology division 20 or 25 years ago. There is no way I was calling him. I remembered a man whose face consisted of hair, a nose and a pair of glasses... He was doing HIV research...it scared me to death at the time...he never smiled once; he looked very somber...

Greg: *The reason I was somber was because I was giving a talk about AIDS and HIV. At the time in1982, there was no cure nor treatment for the disease, so many people were dying from it; it was a very serious topic; I was not smiling...*

Lisa: *At the time, I didn't tell my friend that I knew Greg. The next day he called me up and asked, 'Did you call Greg?' I said, 'No'. He said, 'Get a pencil, write his name down. Greg ...*

Greg: *I was happily married for 35 years; then my wife died of Leukemia. Two years after my wife passed away, I decided to enroll in an online dating site. I created a profile with a preference for widowers, rather than divorcees. Ten days nothing, then all of sudden, I saw this picture of a very beautiful woman. Not only that, she was right for me from every aspect: widow, doctor, right size...I couldn't believe it, so I wrote to her from my computer and asked her whether she would be interested in meeting me for a coffee...Within 10 minutes, I got the answer back, 'No.' Then about five minutes later, I got another email from the same person, saying, 'Maybe sometime in the future.' I said, 'Oh, just forget about it.' I put that out of my mind...*

Lisa: *After two weeks went by, I took a chance and contacted his profile on the dating site 'I still look like my picture. Are you still interested in coffee?' After a couple of back and forth messages between us, he signed one of them 'Greg" and then, the light bulb went on in my head. OMG! This must be the same Greg I knew him way back. So I wrote him an email saying that my friend had said we'd get along so well together and I was really looking forward to meeting him. I clicked 'send' and immediately thought, 'what if that wasn't Greg, I was sure we'd get along well and was looking forward to meeting him. I clicked 'send' again. It turns out, he responded. I was right the first time. Then I found his name and his home address in the phone book. We lived just a few blocks away from each other...*

Greg: *Then we met. I found out we had lots of similarities. First, I found out her maiden name... It was the same as my mother's maiden* *name. Then she told me her other ancestral names. I thought it was very interesting because when I was in college, my freshman organic chemistry professor was a very famous scientist at Harvard University; Lisa said that was her cousin who was the chief of neurosurgery. Also, I had a well-renowned professor who was chief neurosurgery. Lisa said, 'Oh, he is also my cousin'...Lisa's father was a research scientist and pediatrician and I worked at Children's Hospital, also a researcher... We had lots in common...*

Lisa: *After we dated a few times, I wanted to show Greg a bench in the Forest Park where my late husband's colleagues had placed in his memory, overlooking the fountain. It is the most beautiful part of the park...*

Greg: *I told Lisa that in Forest Park people from my work also planted a tree for my late wife; it was a beautiful legacy. So we drove to the park. I followed her directions to turn right, turn left ... as we got closer, I realized we were headed for the tree that my colleagues planted for my late wife. When we were getting closer, I realized what was happening ... Once we got to her bench, my wife's tree was right behind Lisa's husband's bench.*

Lisa: *It was SO strange! We both were standing there, so dumbstruck... Seriously? It was unbelievable!*

Greg: *This was a bashert moment. We are meant to be.*

At that moment, the phrase we Chinese use to define the meaning of "bashert" came to me:

* ***An invisible red thread connects those who are destined to meet, regardless of time, place, or circumstance. The thread may stretch or tangle, but will never break.***

Thanking Those Who Came Before Us

The first time I met them, It was a very moving and inspirational event. It might not have happened without the help of my daughter, Helen. She worked at Washington University as a fundraiser. Her job was to raise money for medical research. One day I got an unusual phone call from her office.

"Mom, could you cook a meal for a party of 10 guests at a doctor's home?"

Before I could give my one and only daughter a "No" -- because it had been 25 years since I last catered a dinner -- Helen explained why she volunteered me.

"Mom, you would love this couple, Dr. Lisa and Dr. Greg! Dr. Lisa at Washington University wants to honor her mentor, Dr. Eisen, for his outstanding professional character. Isn't that cool?"

"Who is Dr. Eisen? Who is Dr. Lisa? Me, doing what?" I was not sure what a Chinese meal had to do with private fundraising. Helen explained:

"Dr. Lisa has great admiration for her mentor, Dr. Eisen, because he always nurtures and encourages his medical fellow residents, and because he is dedicated to medical science. Lisa is trying to raise funds to honor him with an endowment fund which he doesn't know about. The plan is for those who have been significant donors to the fund to tell him at a very special festive dinner...

...These funds are to be used as travel honoraria for young doctors and scientists to present their work at meetings. He was just asked to come to a dinner at Dr. Lisa's house. Nothing more. These five couples are all doctors who have donated significant amounts of money. Each one has been influenced by Dr. Eisen directly. Each gave money for this fund under Dr. Eisen's name...

...The hosts of the party, both Dr. Lisa and her husband, Dr. Greg., love and appreciate authentic Chinese food. Mom, since you like to cook Chinese meals and entertain Americans by telling them the stories behind each dish, I thought.. if you wouldn't mind doing..."

I was very touched by my daughter's special request. After listening to Helen's description of the people involved, I gave my one and only daughter a definite "Yes."

After her request, I did some research to learn about Dr. Eisen's contribution to the field of medical science.

Dr. Eisen

He was a professor and recruited from Harvard Medical School and the Massachusetts General Hospital to be the chief of Dermatology at Washington University School of Medicine from 1967 to 1996. His contributions to medicine have been formally recognized by awards from the National Institutes of Health and the Society for Investigative Dermatology.

On that special evening, I prepared eight courses. Every dish was brought in one at a time to the formal dining room table. As each dish was served, I talked briefly about its origin and shared cultural tidbits or stories.

At the end of the meal, each guest gave a speech that touched my heart profoundly. One of the female dermatologists started:

"He treats every patient who gets into the room the same. It doesn't matter whether you are a multimillionaire or the poorest person; he treats the patient exactly the same with the utmost respect. That is his number one rule. He is totally dedicated to delivering excellent care! He trains doctors to be the best clinician or the best scientist...his training is the most nurturing, the kindest, and the most positive experience any clinician can ever have...Once you were there, you were expected to work hard, but constantly encouraged to learn...His name is Dr. Eisen."

Her speech was so authentic, so sweet, so special... much sweeter than the Eight Treasures Rice Pudding I made for dessert on that special night. The entire evening, people were acknowledging how important Dr. Eisen had been in their lives. It was inspiring.

After the party, I invited Dr. Lisa and Dr. Greg to my humble house for a family meal. I wanted to express my admiration for them as a couple and how they showed their respect for their teacher. I learned more about this loving and respectful couple.

Dr. Lisa

Dr. Lisa had followed Dr. Eisen for five years after medical school. Each year, she donated money to honor him and show him how much she appreciated what he had taught her.

Why?

"Otherwise I wouldn't be doing what I am doing because of his nurturing and encouraging. This year I wanted to make it more than the usual amount...so I came up with the idea. We wanted to do something meaningful for clinical medicine and science since Dr. Eisen is so dedicated to teaching both...

...it is so perfect for fellows who travel to a meeting, or who have written about an unusual case or research -- they can travel with their expenses paid."

When the word "dermatology" is mentioned, pimples or acne come to my mind first. Yet, what I learned from Dr. Lisa was:

"Dermatology is not just about skin. Oh, no! It's not just pimples or acne. It is serious disease. There is skin cancer. For us, some serious infections can have a skin manifestation. Then there are chronic skin diseases."

She made me think about how my entire family has darker skin than most Chinese. While growing up, friends sometime teased us, saying that we might not really be Chinese. I asked her about skin tone. She explained:

"In general, darker skin actually has a more protective pigment."

Speaking of Chinese skin, she shared her experiences in China.

"When Greg and I went to China last year and gave a speech to their 11 pediatric dermatologists in the Children's Hospital in Chung Ching, Sichuan province, there were 1,400 beds! It was mind boggling! In America, the largest Children's Hospital is in Texas, where there are 750 beds."

I was totally surprised to learn that she and her husband Dr. Greg traveled to China to help young dermatologists by providing the latest medical research and findings in my country. For me, it was a "bashert" moment. I was grateful.

Dr. Greg and the SPOT Program

Raised in New York, Dr. Greg developed an interest in science and biology at a young age. He also wanted to help people.

"I wasn't really sure what I wanted to do during college... When I graduated from Harvard, the Vietnam War was very active. Toward the end of college, I decided to be an internist. During my residency, there was a program called CDC, Center for Disease Control."

Dr. Greg has been specializing in children's HIV and AIDS at Washington U. for over 20 years. Yet, I have not heard news about children's HIV or AIDS in the city where I have been living since late 70s. He recalled the beginning of the service.

"When I started to take care of patients, they were poor or gay teens or children of drug addicts who were very very sick... Every day, I saw very sick children with very sick parents who were drug addicts...I was totally involved with helping the children with very sick parents...and involved with helping the children with AIDS... I never thought they would grow up...It was a very depressing time to care for innocent children. But now, with years of new medications, very seldom do patients die with AIDS.

Children grow up now." A big smile appeared on his face. Then he paused and continued,

"However, what happens right now is very disturbing! We have seen lots of teenagers who are affected by this disease because they are engaging in unsafe and risky practices..."

Dr. Greg has been very actively involved with prevention through the program called, **SPOT** which stands for **Support Positive Opportunities for Teens**. He dedicates his profession to helping teenagers who are affected by this disease.

He spoke from the heart when I asked him what the solution was.

"First and foremost, we need a vaccine. Second, we need medication for them to take to prevent getting infected. Beyond that, they need lots of education."

Because of Dr. Greg's dedication, I have learned more about The SPOT Program: It is a monthly pediatric HIV support group that includes services from trained professionals like OB/GYNs, social workers, job counselors, and therapists. They also provide the food and transportation. Topics addressed include information on HIV, prevention, trust, self-esteem, and bereavement issues. SPOT now has a mobile unit that can set up on the street and people come in for free tests and education.

My admiration for this loving couple whose dedication to improve and save human lives is beyond any word can be described.

Postscript:

Sometime later in that year, I was invited by Lisa and Greg to attend a special fundraising party at the St. Louis Chase Park Plaza Hotel. Wow!

The event was to raise funds for Lydia's House, a charitable organization that provides safe, affordable, transitional housing for those in need.

Not only did Greg and Lisa treat me to a wonderful dinner and event, but they also enthusiastically bid on some of the goods that were auctioned that night.

I looked over to Lisa, and then to Greg. They illuminated the room with happiness and love -- for each other, their colleagues, and many people near and dear to them yesterday and today.

As Confucius stated:
* *Wisdom, compassion, and courage are the three universally recognized moral qualities of men.*
* *Humanity is the solid foundation of all the virtues.*

Drama Queen

Kim Furlow

When I consider the passion of every artist, I can't help but wonder what makes them want to pursue their craft so intensely. Musicians may spend hours and hours practicing and revising melodies. Yet, to my ears, the original notes sound wonderful. What inspires them to repeatedly fine tune, seek an ever more perfected performance? How do artists turn a variety of sketches into one painting? How do actors maintain the stamina to rehearse the same lines over and over again?

My friend Kim Furlow embraced the stage and the passion of performing at a young age. She is a talented and wonderful performer, but she also has the special gift of teasing out the nuances of a performance and sharing that with the audience.

During her career, she has played many different roles, demonstrating with every entrance onto and exit from the stage that an artist can teach, inspire, and entertain.

In her mother's words, *"She is a Drama Queen!"*

I first met Kim when she was eighteen as she was practicing her singing in the family's living room. She exhibited great emotion and expression. The Furlow family had just moved to Missouri from Louisiana.

During that time, Kim had auditioned for and was hired by Six Flags to perform in the six Broadway musical shows that were produced during the summer season. Kim remembers the role that theater played in her life.

"*It was a total culture shock moving from Louisiana to St. Louis, Missouri. I did get a scholarship to Northeast Louisiana University for Drama, but my family moved to St. Louis...*

...That summer, I had the best job ever working at Six Flags. I made the best, life-long friends during that summer. I still have them today, and they still support me and come to my shows."

Kim has been involved with more than 150 shows since she came to St. Louis. She is the founder and artistic director of Dramatic License Productions, which was located at Chesterfield Mall in St. Louis from 2009 to 2015. Each year the company produced thirty-five shows, including dramas, comedy shows and cabarets. The company lasted six seasons. Kim produced all performances as well as acting and singing in most shows.

Alice in Wonderland

Kim grew up performing, starting in early childhood inspired by Alice in Wonderland.

"*When I was five or six years old, I remembered saying that I wanted to be like Alice, who fell down in the rabbit hole. This was the story of a little girl who was having an incredible set of adventures meeting so many characters. I took great pleasure creating voices for the characters, acting them out, and singing songs for my mother.*"

Kim dreamed big, even as a child. When she was ten, she wanted to be a princess. Of course, other little girls made that wish, too, but Kim actually acted on it. Once she auditioned for the role of a princess in a school play. Although she didn't get that part, yet, she played the princess's dog! With the canine character in mind, she created a fun, energetic, and hilarious character. Everybody in the audience laughed.

She knew then, at the age of ten, that she could make an audience respond to her performance -- and she loved it!

When she played the role of Mae West in the comedy, *Dirty Blonde*, I was in the audience at the Dramatic License Productions' theater at Chesterfield Mall. Kim not only walked, dressed, and acted like the sexy Mae West, but she also delivered the punch lines right on the nose with that famous seductive voice.

Each time Kim delivered one of those famous Mae West lines, she brought the house down:

- *I used to be Snow White, but I drifted.*
- *It is better to be looked over than overlooked.*
- *Marriage is a fine institution, but I'm not ready for an institution.*
- *Good girls go to heaven, bad girls go everywhere.*
- *When I'm good, I'm very good, but when I'm bad, I'm better.*

We were so impressed! These are pretty famous lines, so many of us were anticipating them. Kim used her own unique interpretation and connection with the audience to create uproarious laughter. Her friends, fans, and even first-time audience members flocked to her after the performance and said;

"*Oh my God! That's your forte!*"

Privately, Kim always gives the credit of her success to her mom.

"*I think I got it from my mom. She is pretty funny, always cutting up, joking around, having a good time...My mom would always come to see my plays; she always supports me. It is very important that I have that support from my mom!* "

During my entire teaching career, it was such a pleasure to work with Kim's mom, Sherry, whose specialty was helping visually impaired students. She had great compassion for her students and treated teaching with focus, seriousness, and sincerity. But after school,

Sherry never failed to joke. She always made me laugh, and I think her gifts have inspired Kim.

Kim's mom, Sherry, and I worked for the same school district since the early 80s. That is how I came to know these two ladies and have the good fortune of being in their presence as Kim matured and developed her talent. Throughout the decades of our friendship, I have seen and marveled at how Kim used her talent and passion to become an outstanding performing artist. She has pursued her craft with such focus and has achieved so much, including the creation of a theater in the most unlikely of places.

The Sound of Music

Laughter is not an every-day, every-moment thing. There are moments of reflection, sadness, fear, love, jealousy, compassion, and more. As a little girl, Kim was inspired by the power of musicals to convey these emotions.

"Mom would have her headphones on when she was wrapping Christmas gifts and would sing at the top of her lungs. So many of the songs were from great musicals with amazing stories and characters. Songs like 'Some Enchanted Evening,' and 'Younger Than Spring Time' from South Pacific or 'I Could Have Danced All Night' and 'Wouldn't It Be Lovely' from My Fair Lady, and 'Maria' and 'America' from West Side Story. I remember asking mom 'What are you singing?' "

Kim thinks back to that with a chuckle. *"She really wasn't that great of a singer, but she sure loved to sing, so I was kind of indoctrinated by my mother's own 'sound of music.'"*

As an artistic director, Kim made sure each year that her theater produced two Broadway cabarets and one holiday musical revue, a tribute to her mother's example.

High School Drama Class

While growing up, Kim was very aware that she was a visual learner. Whether it was watching a ballet or a historical scene acted out in a classroom, the visual presentations left their mark.

"Vision stimulates my brain! I will never forget watching the Nutcracker Suite...I was in awe that they used movement - no dialog - to tell a story. I became fascinated with the storytelling through seeing the stage performance."

During her high school years, she especially loved her history teacher, who acted out the scene of Columbus sailing the ocean blue and arriving in America on Oct. 12, 1492.

"I remembered that part of history all because of my history teacher...

*...Also, my drama class teacher, Mrs. Linda Thompson... now deceased... had great impact on me. She was really wonderful! One day, Mrs. Thompson saw me and said, 'You need to audition for **Bye Bye Birdie**.' I did go for the audition and got the part."*

Because of her high school drama teacher's encouragement, she tried another audition for a Broadway musical, called **Two by Two,** at the local theater. The story is about Noah's preparations for the Great Flood and its aftermath. In that musical, there was a female character named Goldie. Kim grinned and said,

"I didn't know Goldie was a prostitute. During the audition, I belted out the songs in my high soprano voice...You know, I could sing the high notes. The director said to me, 'You had the right voice for this part and you are the only one who can hit the high notes so far, but... how old are you?' I said, 'I'm fourteen,' and he said, 'You are only fourteen? I thought you were twenty or something.'...

...Later he told my mom that I looked great, acted great, sang great, but it wasn't appropriate at my age to play that role; however, I did get a bunch

of other leading roles during my high school years. I knew I could act, could sing, could make people laugh... also, that's when I remembered that I wanted to be on the stage...all the lights were whirling around...I love to be on stage acting, singing, and making people laugh!"

Kim can make you respond to all subtle aspects of human emotion, from laughter to tears. When she played the part of Sister Aloysius in John Patrick Shanley's **Doubt**, her performance was captivating. She portrayed a strict nun who confronts Father Flynn, a priest who is suspected of inappropriate behavior with a young male student at a Catholic school. We could feel and sense her character's suspicion and doubt. We could understand the character's compassion for her students coupled with her need to set a strict and regimented set of rules. Nobody in the audience blinked when she and the actor playing the priest had their ultimate stand-off.

*"**Doubt** was nominated for five St. Louis Kevin Kline Awards, including Best Play, Best Ensemble, Best Actor, Best Director, and Best Actress,"* said Kim proudly.

The Steve and DC Radio Talk Show

After graduating from Fontbonne University with a degree in communications, Kim found work at a local radio station because of her vocal talent. Kim could create a variety of characters with her voice.

"The 'Steve and DC' radio show was very popular at the time; it was kind of controversial because nobody had heard of that kind of show. They were crude, rockers, rough...I created voices and characters using different accents. Sometimes I would speak with a strong St. Louis accent on the radio like 'I was driving on Highway Farty-Far this morning...' I was totally silly on the 'Steve and DC' morning talk show at the time."

During those years, her mom and I couldn't wait to talk about what Kim had said on the radio that morning. I was always the one who laughed hardest, but we both would end up with stomachaches from the laughter. Kim's voices were especially funny to me as a Chinese immigrant who had lived in different areas of the country and had tried to adapt to the local accents.

All countries have different accents, and to my ears, America has some pretty unusual accents. When I moved to this country, my first home was in Texas, so as I developed my English language skills, I did so with a Texas twang. I remember visiting my brother, David, in New York. We were at a restaurant in Queens, and he asked me what I wanted to order. I looked at the menu and asked David,

"Do y'all have Fried Okra here in New York?"

A complete look of shock appeared on his face. He stuttered and could only utter a few words. *"Oh, wow, you...you...Texas...oh...wow! "* I was clueless about what he was "wowing" me about. Now, whenever I see Kim playing a southern lady on the stage, I am always there in the audience. I will always enjoy Southern accents and mannerisms.

Southern Women and Steel Magnolias

On July 27, 2012, in the Entertainment section of the St. Louis Post-Dispatch, it read, *"Playing Southern Women is Kim Furlow's forte."* The editor endorsed three different shows in which Kim played three totally different southern women at her Dramatic License Productions' theater at Chesterfield Mall.

Kim played the character of Amanda, the mother of two adult children, in Tennessee Williams' melancholy family drama, **The Glass Menagerie.** In **Steel Magnolias,** she played M'Lynn, the mother of Shelby, who had a serious health issue. And she sang and played Betty, one of a trio of women in **The Great American Trailer Park Musical**. In these three plays, Kim successfully demonstrated talented and passionate portrayals.

As Kim and I discussed these roles, she slipped right into a dramatic Southern accent and said,

"Ayh was born in Germany, but grew up in Louisiana. Let me tell you this, playing Southern characters is the most fun, and Ayh know how they feel... I know some Southern women, and they ain't taking 'no' for an answer, but they sure bond with their women friends real tayhght..."

While listening to her accent as she lightheartedly talked, I couldn't help contrast that with the role she played as the mother in **Steel Magnolias**. As M'Lynn at the wake, she began to accept her daughter Shelby's death. I still remember Kim's heartfelt expression of feeling as a mother who just lost her daughter. Her accent came through loud and clear as she delivered her lines with the broad Southern vowels.

"I find it amusing... Men are supposed to be made out of steel or something. I just sat there. I just held Shelby's hand. There was no noise, no tremble, just peace. Oh God! I realize as a woman how lucky I am. I was there when that wonderful creature drifted into my life and I was there when she drifted out. It was the most precious moment of my life..."

We were sitting in the audience, quietly wiping our tears in the dark.

Dramatic License Productions

With her passion for the performing arts, one might wonder how Kim made the transition from morning radio to opening her own theater at a mall. She said it all began with a fundamental question from deep in her soul.

"What would the world would be like without art?"

Kim is multi-talented with experience in marketing, public relations, public speaking, advertising, event management, creative writing, and social media.

"The companies I had worked with paid me very well, and I saved up a lot because I thought I could use my own savings to promote the arts in West County."

After working on the radio show, Kim formed her own consulting company with her savings, Dramatic License Productions, which works with nonprofit clients.

Since 2004, Kim has poured her heart and soul into promoting the performing arts and making sure that people have access to it. Kim noticed that west of Interstate 270 in St. Louis, there were no real performing arts venues. Therefore, she reached out to the St. Louis Regional Arts Commission, which fosters the arts in St. Louis. Shortly thereafter, she received a call from Chesterfield Mall. They were thinking of taking one wing that was vacated by retailers and turning it into an *"ARTropolis"*, where artists could use the space for their creation! Kim decided to create a theater for the performing arts.

*"In my heart, I thought it would be a great idea to start a professional venue where actors, designers, directors could actually make a living doing what they love to do, right here in St, Louis. They wouldn't have to go to Chicago or New York; they could stay here. **Through the theatre, we could bring to our community a better understanding of history, of human nature... to enhance the lives of many. "***

That was how Dramatic License Productions started. She wanted to connect with people in the community.

"For everyone who has never seen a play...if we can bring the show locally, closer than downtown St. Louis to them...I will do that! I want to be a part of that community."

The meaning behind the name of her production company is plain, simple, and real.

"We like to create things and make them into drama or comedy or musicals. It was a perfect name for this organization - Dramatic License Productions!"

It Takes a Village To Build a Theater

Working with the management team at Chesterfield Mall, Kim grabbed the opportunity. The 1,495 sq-ft space was transformed into a black box theater, seating 85.

Fifty volunteers created and transformed the space by painting walls, sanding woodwork, and installing ceiling tiles. In a record three-month transformation, they were ready for the first show, rehearsals and all!

"We tapped into everybody we knew to help us out...your daughter, Helen, and I worked along with the board of directors to paint 400 ceiling tiles... your Steve helped us to build the wooden risers... we had to put 1,500 pounds of steel bars at the ceiling to hold lighting fixtures that weigh about 75 pounds per piece...everything we did had to pass the county code... we had to put up this huge sound proof curtain..."

Because of the limited stage space, no more than eight performers could be on stage at any one time. Productions included small shows with very compelling scripts that would attract audiences. In many cases, the performances also boosted the local economy like the time a local, professional set designer was hired to build seven doors for the set of ***Boeing, Boeing***.

*"We created about twenty jobs per show each season. Since we do four to six shows a year, we pay them a stipend... you do the math. Personally, I realize that most people who do theater do so for the love for the art, not for the pay. **Personally, I just want everybody in St. Louis to see a play. Everybody who has not seen a play, go see a play!.**"*

Then Kim stopped for few moments and said,

"Actually, I have a bumper sticker on my car that reads, 'Go See A Play.'"

Every performance I attended at the Chesterfield Mall was outstanding. It is with great pride that I will always remember Kim's role in founding and nurturing the theater and its effect on the community.

Kim brought her passion for theater to an area that was lacking in theatrical venues, thus enriching the Chesterfield community in a way that had never been seen before. For Kim, **art should be shared**. She didn't just believe this. She acted on it. With hard work and incredible energy, Kim made a dream come true for the suburban community and enriched many lives in the process.

Postscript

Dramatic License Productions' theater at Chesterfield Mall closed in 2015 and Kim moved on to another projects such as advocacy group for women in theater called, *St. Louis Women in Theater*. What an accomplishment!

* *A bird does not sing because it has an answer. It sings because it has a song.*

An Art-Filled Life with free and generous spirit

Steve Hilton

My friendship with Steve Hilton can best be described by citing an ancient, and very poetic quote: *Friendship is not limited by age nor time.* 友誼長存

We've been friends since the 90's. Neither one of us can recall the first time we met, but we know it was through a circle of mutual friends. Among us, I was the oldest one, and Steve was the youngest. Both of us were high school teachers, and other than that, we had nothing in common, except that we really like to eat and laugh!

Our group of friends enjoyed hanging out together after school. During spring break of 2003, we decided to go skiing in Colorado, lodging at the seminary. It was my first trip to see the spectacular, snow-covered mountain view and to experience a ski trip!

Almost!

Once in Colorado, the group decided that before we skied, we would go ice skating. For some reason, the instructor selected me for a very special position - Observer. I was honored and relieved that I was "excused" from actual skating. Steve, on the contrary, did not need any instruction, gliding along the shiny ice with ease.

I was such a skilled observer that I continued in this role over the next few days as the group skied down the mountain. In addition to my observer responsibilities, I became official Coffee Taster. During the evenings, the group gathered together in the lodge with the moon shining brightly over us as we shared wonderful stories. We had a blast!

On every bus ride home, Steve and I chatted and teased each other as usual. Anyone looking at us might have thought that we were the "odd couple". Then out of the blue, Steve asked,

"Hey Lou! " He always calls me 'Lou'. *"Ahhh...do you have any...ahh... advice for me?"* I couldn't tell whether he was joking or serious.

*"**Teachers open the door, you enter by yourself.**"* I gave him the words of wisdom.

"Did you just make that up? Or did you steal it from Confucius?"

"Confucius said it."

"Ahhh, Lou! What about you?" He questioned me with a semi serious attitude, I answered him wholeheartedly;

"Teaching is my passion! Whether it's helping smart and defiant teenagers with math or teaching adults about Chinese cooking."

I wondered if he was asking me for advice about his work or his life.

Connoisseurship of Chinese Cuisine

At the time, Steve taught science at Ladue High School. Some weekends, he would come over to my house and watch me cook. After many moons, he became my "guinea pig". It started with a dinner party at home. One of my new dishes was a Chinese salad which received raving reviews. But I was afraid my American friends were just being polite, so I asked Steve for his honest opinion. Without hesitation, he said,

"Ahhh! Lou... this is a bit salty!"

After that honest feedback, I wanted him know that he was always welcome to taste my food. But, first, he needed to learn how to use chopsticks to eat. To pass my "chopstick test," he had to pick up a peanut with chopsticks. He sure passed the test effortlessly.

From that point on, when I would review for the newspaper or food magazine, he and I would go to Chinese restaurants once or twice a month. Our friendship continued to grow, and our bond was very much like an "auntie and nephew."

One day, I got an unexpected request to cater a dinner for a good friend who wanted to celebrate her husband's birthday. Steve came to my mind; I knew I could count on him. Immediately, he said,

"Lou, What do you want me to do? I will be your servant, busboy or slave...whatever!"

"You be the 5 Star General and I'll be the Commander in Chief." I replied.

"Ahhh...Commander In Chief! Are you making General Tso's Chicken for the party?"

My first catering job was a great success! Our strategy worked flawlessly as we cooked, taste-tested, plated, garnished, and presented all of the dishes. The rotation worked well too, with dishes being retrieved and cleaned in a timely manner. The 5-star General and Commander-in-chief were a great team.

Act of Kindness

One day, out of the blue, Steve invited me to the Central West End to listen to music. After the performance was over, as he was ready to drive me home, he suddenly asked me to stay in the car. I saw him hurry across the street and walk up to an odd looking man. Steve patiently listened to this bearded middle age person, wearing ragged clothes. I watched closely as Steve gave this stranger his full attention while occasionally nodding. I was getting impatient and started to worry about Steve, I was ready to blow the horn. Suddenly, Steve ran toward the car. He jumped in, and I asked him about the strange guy. As he started the car, Steve anxiously said,

"Let's get out of here! Let's go! Quick!"

"Where? What happened? What's wrong?" I was alarmed and frightened.

Steve didn't utter a word but totally focused on driving. Suddenly, he stopped the car, got out, and ran toward the Subway Sandwich store. Meanwhile, I saw the stranger run toward the store and wait outside. Then, I knew what Steve was doing. The stranger was a homeless man. After Steve came back into the car, he explained,

"He asked me to give him the money to buy food. I told him I would give him food, but not money. He agreed, then I asked him to meet me at the Subway. That's the end of the story."

"But, why did you have to run?"

"'Cause he was very hungry! "

********* ********* *************

Steve is an easy going kind of guy. Nothing would get him upset in this materialistic world. One day, I was very surprised to see him getting very frustrated over some thing on the way to school. He kept saying he couldn't comprehend what people were thinking. Finally he let out his frustration; I listened.

"There is this guy who walks on the same street as I drive to school every single day, same time… it is a pretty long way. Every morning, I see him get off the bus and walk on the same road. I always open my door and say, 'Hey, I'll give you a ride, come on in…' but, he never accepts my offer.

This has been going on for a long time. I just don't get it... And...then today, it was raining, pouring down... When I saw him, I quickly stopped my car and opened the door, shouting, 'Hey, get in here. I will take you wherever you work, get inside...don't walk in the rain...

...For the first time, he finally accepted my offer today! I took him to where he works which turned out to be just down a block from my school...he could have had a ride from the bus to where he works everyday... I don't get why people are so stubborn...wouldn't accept help!"

"What does he do?" I asked.

"Works at a restaurant...Who cares?"

"Is he Chinese? Black? Latino? White? " I thought for a while, then jokingly I asked.

"What difference does it make?"

Special Meaningful Gifts

Steve Hilton was a high school science teacher, taught a variety of science topics from environmental science, astronomy, oceanography to earth science. On Saturdays, he taught ceramics in his high school art studio.I would occasionally watch him teaching this class... it was fascinating! One day, I asked,

"How did you start teaching ceramics?"

He stopped the pottery wheel, pointing to the school ceramics teacher, Vic Bassman who was working on the other side of the studio; Steve said,

"Vic teased me constantly, saying 'Come make pots, come make pots, you will really like it' and my answer was always, 'Nope!' until one day he said, 'Steve, you are a cheapskate... you will never have to buy another

Christmas gift if you would just come make some pots.' thirty seconds later, I was addicted to clay...till today!"

Little did he know then ....thousands of ceramic pots later... he, too would be a ceramics professor with art exhibits around the world.

While Steve was learning from Vic how to make pottery, he asked me one day to write *"Friendship"* in Chinese, so he could copy it. Weeks later, he brought me a shinning brown flower pot, and on the front were green-colored Chinese characters representing, *'Friendship'*. His gift touched me forever. And this beautiful gift still has a special place on my deck.

After this special gift, more to follow. On a trip to Central America with his Ladue High School students, he returned with ideas for new creations: six hand made lantern sculptures. Five of the lanterns had sad facial expressions carved and glazed on their tops. I was amazed but bewildered. So, I asked him about the sad faces. He said,

"I saw abject poverty, people were doing everything possible including ruining their habitats, to feed and clothe their families! It is same thing we did here in this country in the 1700's and 1800's/

Flower pot with "Friendship"

After Steve gave me these six hand made lanterns, I placed one in my front yard and five sad faces lanterns in each of my four miniature gardens: Chinese vegetable section, Japanese Zen plot, New Mexico fire pit, and French vineyard area.

Sad face lantern   **Lantern in the front yard**

Steve's hand sculptured lanterns are placed in between from East to West in these gardens at my home. As the seasons change, the lanterns sit among the flowers to connect the love and friendship from China to America. During Chinese Mid-Autumn Festival, I light candles in the lanterns during dinner parties. The lanterns he made remind me that Steve is expressing his ideology of connecting civilizations without sacrificing tradition. Thanks to his remarkable sensitivity, I feel grateful! His creative artwork is deeply appreciated.

Central America

Steve took students to Central America not once, but three times. I had to know what made this science teacher so dedicated, so I asked;

"What were you doing there in Central America during the year of 1994-1996?"

"We went to study culture and ecology. Our first trip was to Costa Rica. The following year in Belize, 18 students obtained their diving certifications and we explored the underwater beauty of the barrier reef, 30 km from Columbia. It's one of the most isolated places in Central America."

71

Steve has also sailed in the North Atlantic, worked on research vessels in the Gulf of Mexico. He even took a summer job by running a dive shop in Tonga in the South Pacific.

What for? I wondered.

"I wanted to be able to tell students stories of living science instead of having them read it out of a book."

The Perfect Match

Steve's insatiable, intellectual mind and unlimited creativity soon made him feel the need for a new adventure. While he was searching for different possible routes, as a fluke, he discovered a flyer in his mail box describing a new program at Missouri State University. A graduate assistant was needed.

Steve called, but was told that he had to be a current art teacher. Since he had been teaching ceramics for three years on every Saturday, the university official replied,

"Well... Sounds like a loophole! When can you come?"

He took a sabbatical leave from his teaching job at high school as a science teacher and pursued his Master Degree in Art Education with an art certification at MSU. That's where he met a girl named Alissa who was pursuing the same degree.

After graduation, they both ended up teaching at Ladue High School. At that time, Steve was teaching ceramics, sculpture, drawing, computer animation, graphic design and optical art. Alissa was doing her student teaching. After seeing what a great teacher she was, Ladue High School hired Alissa!!! Steve agreed that she should 'take over' his art classes, which 'forced' him back into the science classroom.

"But it ended up OK." With a big smile, Steve said, *"She became my wife!"*

Here Come the Bride and the Groom!

Steve and Alissa got married in Hawaii and invited the immediate family to attend their wedding on the beach. Both bride and groom wore shorts and T-shirts on their wedding day. Steve said,

"Both of us had shorts on, but Alissa's shorts were cut-off jeans and we both wore sandals."

After the wedding, the garden party reception was celebrated back at Alyssa's parents home in Town and Country. Like all the other guests, we were anxious to see the bride and the groom. The music started to play, and what a sight!

Thirty of the groom's best friends came out wearing soccer shorts and Ladue High School soccer T - shirts. Then, came the bride and the groom. Holding hands with his new bride, Steve grinned a genuine, unpretentious, but a mischievous smile. Both were wearing shorts and happily chatting with their guests.

This loving couple made a commitment that from that day forward: all life's decisions would be based on ***mutual support and agreement*** on their life together.

Snowboarding from Utah to Alaska

After the few years later, Alissa and Steve decided to leave St. Louis and headed for Taiwan to teach English. On their way, they traveled through Salt Lake City and stopped to do some snowboarding. Someone complimented them on their boarding skills and said that they both would be good at teaching snowboarding. Instead of going to Taiwan, they decided to teach snowboarding for two years at Brighton, Utah.

"After that, it was Alissa's turn to decide where we should go. She picked Alaska!"

Steve said.

"*What did you do in Alaska?*" I asked.

"*I taught 7th grade science and ceramics for a year while I was deciding to see where I was going to complete my second graduate degree.*"

"*Teaching science, not snowboarding in Alaska?*" I asked.

"*Yep!* " Steve said. "*After Alaska, I have been all 50 states, Alaska is the most beautiful state.*"

College Professor and Exhibiting Artist

During a year of solitude in Alaska, Steve spent time thinking about his career path. He decided he wanted to pursue his Master's degree in Fine Art. The following year, he ended up in Tempe, Arizona, where he eventually received his MFA in ceramics. This allows him to teach at the university level.

"*Lucky for me, I have an incredible wife who shares my passion for art. She has given me the ultimate gift for allowing me to 'quit life' and earn my MFA. Without her support, the emotional and financial strain of day-to- day living would have been too difficult.*"

Thanks to Alissa's support, Steve has become a professor of Ceramics and Art Education at Midwestern State U. in Wichita Falls, Texas. As an exhibiting artist and teacher, he travels the world: Portugal, Thailand, Spain, China, Japan, Korea, Cuba, Austria, England and Romania. Many of his art work are permanently displayed in museums and universities across the United States and abroad.

St. Louis Community College Gallery

In 2005, he invited me to preview his art show at Meramec Community College. The day before the public opening, I thought he might need my help, but as I entered the exhibit area, I was immediately impressed.

Steve had sketched a blue outline on the floor, circle here and there like clouds in the sky or waves on the ocean; real sand was filled inside the blue circles.

Steve and Alissa, along with other helpers were patiently putting literally thousands of pieces of broken clay on the floor, piece by piece. Some piled up like small mountain, others were like a running river. When it was done, his "art" appeared to be randomly placed on the floor, however, it also showed a kind of pattern of art work, which I couldn't pinpoint.

During the break, I asked Steve how and where he did all this phenomenal art work. He explained,

"These are all of my broken fired pieces. I carried them in trash bags from exhibit to exhibit. I will keep using them until they are no more than the smallest of pieces. As I move them from place to place, they will erode just like the rocks that crumble with them..."

"Then, why is this work titled, 8,629...8,630...do you really have that many pieces?"

"Oh, this is an inside joke on how many pieces there are...8,629...8,630... as if I counted every one."

"But, what does it mean to you?"

"I hope it is a way for the audience to see the world in a different way. The piece is named so the viewer can bring what they see to it. The meaning is different for everyone. I try to name pieces to bring more meaning to the table. Perhaps a little 'natural' beauty to a world with a

lot of things they are not so beautiful. I am hopeful that the paradigm of shock art is coming to a close."

In 2016, Steve came back to St. Louis for his art workshow, titled *"**Equilibrium**"* (shown at right) with a collaboration over 200 Meramec college math, science and art students.

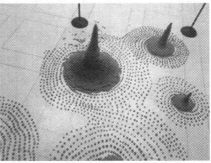

"Why" In Cuba?

Each of his art work that are displayed has title. I find it fascinating! But, over the past few years, he has used the same title, that's one word only, *'**Why**'*. He said it was because he wanted us to ask why. In thinking about his trip to Cuba, he asked,

"Why has there been an embargo going on for the past 60 years?"

He uses unfired clay because of the lack of possibilities in Cuba and to get away from what we take for granted here in the US.

"Why do you think that way?" I asked.

"There has always been water coming out of the spigot, gas coming out *of the stove, electricity coming out of the wall, and we use these resources like there will never be an end to them. In Cuba, and around the world, few are lucky to have just one of the three at any given time."*

While I was in deep thought about what his reasoning, he paused and looked at me, a mischievous smile appeared on his face, he then asked;

"Ahh... Lou, any more questions?"

"He who asks is a fool for five minutes, but he who does not ask *remains a fool forever!"* I replied.

"Did Confucius say that too?"

Teapots Made in China

As an emerging, world renown ceramic artist, Steve Hilton has been invited to China four times by different groups, including the Ceramic Magazine Editors Association. During two of the trips, Steve and Alissa created art for a month as artists-in-residence. Their goal was to influence students and communities. They made teapots in China.

"The greatest number of teapot pieces I have made in China is 50. They were made by folding clay over and over and cutting off the edges, then taking the cuttings and adding them to the top of the pieces just like one would make a coil pot, except my coil is not smooth. They were all fired clay or stoneware to be more accurate, then stained. There is no glaze."

"How long does it take?"

"The teapot pieces takes about 2 to 5 hours... then, there are some of the other 'multiple- piece' works that take months to make up to a year to finish. For some of the pieces, it took a week, and some of the exhibitions took a year to prepare 5 to 7 people working on them at one time. Some of the exhibitions took a year or more to prepare and included teapots that had been 'reworked' to get just the right balance."

"How did you show your 50 teapots? On a large dinning room table in the Art Gallery?"

"On the wall of the Dao Art Space of Xian, China." He answered.

"Not on the Great Wall of China?"

"No, not on the Great Wall of China, these 50 teapots were hung on the wall of the museum... Yea, we did visit the Great Wall and thought it was a pretty cool experience. But, have to say that we had a much better time in the back alleys of some of the cities or towns we were in...eating the

food that people have been eating for thousands of years. We traveled mostly southeastern part of China, from Peking,...to Shanghai and Hong Kong. We ate lots of Peking ducks in between."

Speaking of Peking Duck, I couldn't help by asking my former "5-Star General" about the food over China.

"There is not a better place for food!! Of course you taught me about that!! It is all very different from Chinese food that one gets here in the United States, but we enjoyed the experience! As well as a lot of socialization that goes with eating out. We were usually invited as guests, which meant too damn much food, but when we ate on the street . . . Yum . . . Yum!! My mouth is watering thinking about the dumplings, and "finger" street food..."

Japanese Bamboo Art Show

In 2010, Steve Hilton participated in a show in Futsu, Japan alongside 11 international artists. Their artwork was created on site over a two week period and then shown at the Makki Corporation Gallery.

During that time, Steve was asked to do a residency in Japan and he was told that he would be provided with a kiln and clay, but they turned

out to be in an inconvenient location. So he decided to use materials that were plentiful. Bamboo came to his mind.

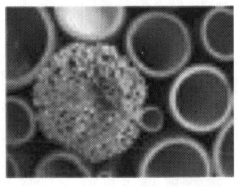

He started work by first cutting down 200 bamboo trees out of the jungle, about 75 to 100 feet tall. He cut them into 20 inches pieces with a chop saw, then sanded, cleaned them to obtain an even color. The small branches were cut to make bundles that fit inside the larger pieces. This was his reason;

"Even the small bamboo pieces are an important part of the 'whole'. Individual parts have to exist to make up what we think we see. When in reality, if it were not for the 36th bamboo piece from the left and 4th from the top, the piece would not be the same...

...As insignificant as we sometimes feel, even the person who thinks he or she has not accomplished anything, in fact, changed the world.... We have a precious place in the present and we will have made a difference in the future."

After listening to his analogy, in my mind I digest his explanation word by word.

Because Steve Hilton has been to many countries, I was very curious about his personal experiences in each culture especially in Japan.

"I learned that there are a lot of very beautiful places in Japan especially in the northern most island."

What about the people?

"Their kids spend too much time in school and they are allowed to walk around 10 pm without supervision... most Japanese are very polite and soft spoken...but they do like to drink! Since we don't drink, I almost starved while there!"

What happened?

"The people we hung around with liked to drink, but neither one of us drinks. Most of the places we ate were bars with food. Even my Japanese friends would order appetizers with five pieces for seven or eight people sitting at the table. According to their culture, no one eats the last piece, so there were only 4 pieces to eat on each plate..."

"Weren't you always hungry?"

"Yep! It took a week or so for me to just be the 'rude' American who eats that last piece."

The Mind of An Artist

As an artist, a former science teacher and geologist, one day, Steve Hilton shares his fundamental philosophy about life. He said,

*"I **have developed an appreciation for the anomalies in many forms of life, in the rock and soil covering the Earth's landscape. I am intrigued by the way plants, animals, and weather influence the Earth's surface by both erosion and deposition. This fascination has become an integral part of my art.**"*

What fascinated me the most is Steve's artistic arrangement of thousands of broken pieces of clays and rocks. It appears to be random but there is "something" indescribable in the logic or pattern that create this incredible phenomenal and beautiful art work.

One time during our conversation about art and science, I asked Steve whether it had anything to do with the math formula in Mario Livio's book, *The Story of Phi* where he developed the theory regarding the mysterious relationship between numbers and the natural of reality. Steve said,

*"Are you kidding? Hey Lou, I still think about the order of the world around us in a mathematic sense. I don't really understand math in that whether there is a formula, but it isn't the actual math that interests me. It's based on the idea of factual: **Everything in a dynamic system is self similar to other things**. In other words, even the way we congregate in a room is fractal, just like a very small piece of broccoli is like the entire plant."*

Down-To-Earth Home, Sweet Home!

Many years ago, Steve's parents invited me to visit their house in Reeds Spring, Missouri. Before arriving at his house, Steve hinted to me that their home was a "family project", a down-to-earth kind of place.

Why and how?

I didn't know what to expect. It was, and still is, the one and only earthen home I have ever seen in my entire life. Steve explained to me;

"To save energy is the main reason. The house has three sides underground and a passive solar panel in the front, facing south, and a 12 ft glass porch."

"How does it save the energy?"

"In the winter, the glassed-in area would get up to 60 degrees on a sunny day, even if it's 10 degrees outside. In the summer, the porch is shaded by the overhanging roof...

...inside the house was eclectic."

"What does that mean, eclectic?"

"Everything we used was collected from all over the world from crystal chandeliers to Thai-carved wooden screen. All the design was done in such a way that we could have someone live with us and still have privacy. "

In my memory, it was the most intriguing house, built from **idealism, scientific experiment,** and **family unity.** Recently during our visit, Steve and I were reminiscing about the house, he provided more detail. This time, I learned more about this unique family.

His father designed the structure, Steve and his brother helped to build this house with their hands. When they started working together as a family project, Steve said that no one predicted that this down-to-earth home would have taken them for literally three decades. Steve was in deep thought and said,

"Our house was actually started in 1986 and finished in 2010. Exactly 3 days before dad died. We used to tease him while we were working together that the day he finished the house, he would be finished. Literally! Like he knew it was time for him to go."

It is an admirable family project built by father and sons. Even though it took nearly 25 years to finish, Steve's father's idea was achieved by building a house based on the belief at saving the energy and preserving the natural environment. Most importantly, his father's spirit has passed on to his sons, greater and wider. It reminds me of one Chinese proverb, which exemplifies what Steve has accomplished in his life.

* Tell me and I will forget; show me and I may remember; involve me and I'll understand.

I know his father would be very proud of what Steve has accomplished. He is an incredible talented artist who uses his scientific background to create extraordinary pieces by using ordinary materials. His art work has travelled all over the world and serves as testament to his free and generous spirit. Steve does not see the world or ethnic difference, but does see the multi-faceted beauty of nature and he strives to preserve it to make the material world pure. This is Steve's gifts to the world as Confucius said:

*   *The superior man is modest in his speech but exceeds in his actions.*

*   *Everything has beauty, but not everyone sees it.*

Don't Rush Past The Simple Wonders

Kent Burgess

Kent Burgess handed me a 4-by-6-inch color photo. The picture was a close-up of two tiny soft yellowish mushrooms in the sharp green grass. The title of the photo was printed at the bottom: *Don't Rush Past the Simple Wonders.* It was his Christmas card, featuring his artwork. Then, he showed me two more. One pictured three raindrops caught on the edge of a bright orange yellow flower; and another captured a spectacular scene of a sunset. He loves the simple things in nature. Every one of his photos zero in on one theme only, focusing on nature as we see it everyday.

Currently, his photos are the centerpieces of the Webster Groves' Club for Wild Life Art Exhibit. This time, the center point of his photo artwork is birds – red tail hawks and bald eagles: flapping their wings, preparing to land, catching a mole, or resting on treetops. Kent took about 150 pictures to catch these few precious moments.

Talented photographer

Where did he take these beautiful images?

"I often watch the sunset at Big Bend and Highway 141. On this particular day, I was wearing a black jacket and black pants and was leaning against the light pole on the top of hill. While I was taking pictures of the sunset, flocks of red-tail hawks suddenly appeared at the far end of the sky. My index finger instantly started to click away. As the birds flew closer and closer in my direction, the clicking was getting faster and faster...

... I caught one hawk swooping down fast, landing, and within seconds, it pulled a mole out of the grass. The next instant that tiny mole was dangling from the mouth of a jealous hawk...

...Then, out of the blue, another hawk was flying directly toward me. It looked like it was approaching the ground. Instead, his eyes were aimed directly at the lens of my camera. A quick snap caught his 'aggressive predator' look. At that moment, I must say I was very intimidated by that hawk's aggression -- animal instinct."

As I was looking at the red-tail hawk's eyes in the picture while Kent was explaining, I couldn't help but thinking to myself: *Run, run, run!*

Kent had expertly captured the emotion of that moment. After showing me pictures of red-tail hawks, he pulled out a picture of two bald eagles. One was perched at the top of the tree, and the other was observing from a lower branch. Kent asked,

"Guess which one is the boss or the father?" Unable to answer, Kent helped me and pointed to the one on the lower branch.

"This one holds the power; he teaches the young eagle at the top of the tree how to gain life skills."

Kent smiled and nodded his head. He was in a reflective mood.

"Watching those wild birds in the sky, as an unscripted nature scene unfolds, reminds me of O'Donohue's saying, 'Animals have a native closeness to the earth and they move in the sure rhythm of this belonging.' This shows the dignity of animals. They enjoy an inner composure and coherence. Animals have fluency of presence."

Who is John O'Donohue?

"John O'Donohue wrote the book "The Beauty". He answered.

Surprisingly, my memory survived and came back instantaneously. Oh yeah! Three years ago, when we met as usual, Kent excitedly suggested that I read O'Donohue's book. The very next day I bought it. Before I even read the first sentence of the first chapter, my soul was totally captivated by the title and subtitle: *The Call of Beauty: The light alone gives grace and truth to life's unquiet dream. EVERY LIFE IS BRAIDED WITH LUMINOUS MOMENTS.*

I asked Kent what his favorite O'Donohue saying was, and without hesitation, he responded,

"The beauty of nature is often the wisest balm for it relieves and releases the caged mind.... O'Donohue was an Irish priest and a philosopher. He died suddenly at the age 52 in 2008. Amazingly, I am still reading his book today! It is a beautiful book. He was also a poet. I especially love this poem, 'Fluent'

> *I would love to live like a river flow*
> *Carried along by the surprise*

Ever since the day I discovered the O'Donohue's book three years ago, the first thing I do in the morning is to read *The Beauty*. Sitting on my deck, I savor one or two pages at a time. Each picturesque sentence creates a painted natural scene that begs an answer to some hidden philosophical question that is quietly knocking on my soul. More often than not, I close the book to reflect while contemplating the Zen garden in my back yard.

Passionate garden designer

Interestingly, my tiny Zen garden was actually inspired by Kent's own Japanese garden. His creation begins in his front yard and wraps around his house: a lovely trail of small, grayish-white stones, his extensive collection of Japanese maples of all sizes and colors, along with a diverse variety of other plants. His hand-made Japanese lantern accent his hand-crafted pots, all of it working together to create a delight for the eyes. The leaves on the Japanese maple trees in his garden are similar, but slightly different.

"Are those Japanese maples basically either green or red varieties?" I asked. *"There are 60 different kinds here."* He pointed at his yard. Kent's love for nature is deep in his heart and is naturally displayed in his Japanese garden.

The Japanese lantern that he handmade is under the maple tree in my Zen Garden. It is a gift from him. (Left)

What a view to see!

Decades of Friendship

Over the years, Kent and I met every six weeks. Nearly thirty years ago, I was a middle-aged Asian woman who told jokes with a strong Chinese accent; Kent, a young American guy who bashfully laughed and listened. As the years have gone by, our roles slowly changed. I have become his faithful listener as Kent articulates his philosophy based on life experience and study.

In his speech, no unrecognizable or fancy words are used; however, his thoughts always call my mind to a deeper meaning. Frequently, I find myself asking him to elaborate.

One day, it just dawned on me that there is a famous Chinese proverb that perfectly describes Kent:

* *Deep thinker, speaks simple.*

To capture these special moments and the pearls of thought, a tape recorder was the perfect solution. Throughout the years of listening, I've collected very special quotes from him:

Deep Thinker

Nowadays, conversation is rare. What passes, as conversation would be better described as intersecting monologue! This is especially true in regards to politics and religion.

Too often we are experiencing our thoughts instead of experiencing the actual moment through our senses first.

Mindfulness is our greatest witness in regard to a life of living free and at peace.

We really don't think anymore or exercise freedom; instead we run on pre-rigged rails of thought others have defined for us.

Freedom is not just a dream. It is there, beyond those fences that we build all by ourselves.

Focus on individual change instead of changing the world. This is the best way to see the world change.

True philosopher

Kent's focus on individual changes has been inspired by many people, one being the French philosopher Jacques Ellul, who was a sociologist, law professor, lay theologian. Again this was the first time I had heard about Jacques Ellul,

*"Among all Jacques Ellul's sayings, '**Think globally, act locally**' really resonated with me."* Kent said.

I admit that the name, Jacques Ellul did not register with me, even though Sociology was my major in my undergraduate school and we studied many philosophers at Taiwan University. Kent was silent, contemplating for a while, then he articulated his thoughts:

*"**All we have is the moment; the past is gone and the future is nothing more than imagined and uncertain. That's why we should act locally, mindfully in each moment.** Jacques Ellus's thinking had a transformative effect on me. One of his major themes is the threat to human freedom created by modern technology. I haven't read all his fifty eight books, but without a doubt his philosophy has definitely influenced my way of thinking."*

Both of us were in thoughts for a while, then my inquisitive mind went back to Kent.

"What is Jacques Ellul's belief or philosophy that triggered your study?"

*"**We really don't think anymore or exercise freedom; instead we run on pre-rigged rails of thought others have defined us**....And these are*

some of the things I have learned through it all. What interested me was Ellul's fundamental theory: The technological tyranny over humanity...."

Out of my own insecure curiosity, emails were sent to Paris, France the following day. My three intelligent and well-educated nieces were born and raised in Paris. The answer from them, who are married to French men, was, *"Auntie Theresa, Jacques Ellul is not a familiar name amongst average French intellects..."*

Wise and Loving Father

During this time with his wife raising three teenage daughters, we discussed these important parenting skills. Using his own experiences, Kent's expressed and demonstrated how he, as a father, had to face inevitable challenging life issue.

`Nothing is more powerful than the transforming presence of love,** **acceptance, and grace**. *If we, as parents use pure force, it might be quicker but it is never as effective. All that does is change external behavior. I want my daughters to see their minds or hearts and how they interact with others. We are living in a society, a culture that is very 'scripted' on how to think, to behave, and to love. For me, life is to be guided not by law, but the spirit. If I use law with the hopes of changing their behavior, mostly all I have done is encouraged them to be more skill at hiding. I rather see them live openly and authentically.... watch them grow into healthy individuals finding their own way."*

Being a teacher all my life, I wholeheartedly respect parents like him.

Soul Searcher

On several occasions he told me that his spiritual awakening started at the age of 42. It was one of the most significant moments in his life.

Fourteen years ago, Kent was at a crossroad with organized religion and freedom of spirituality. Through his friends, he connected with Wayne Jacobsen, a nationally recognized specialist, using meditating to resolve cultural and religious conflicts. After reading one of Jacobsen's books, *The Naked Church*, Kent began to do some soul searching.

"Wayne is a native Californian who is a pastor, writer and a teacher; he travels the world helping Christians to live the life of Christ. Because of Wayne's beliefs, and his book, The Naked Church, I have learned to switch my way of thinking and ask myself,

'Am I a passive follower or an active participant?'"

Genuine humanitarian

In 2010, Kent went to Kenya to put into practice Jacobsen's teachings. While in Kenya for three weeks with Wayne & other American Christian volunteers, Kent helped to build a water structure to allow villagers to wash clothes and food without having to go to the river. He also participated in the building of an orphanage for children whose parents had either died of HIV or in tribal warfare.

"It was not easy to witness how poor they were; they practically had nothing to live on, no place to sleep...they were just kids.... some areas of the town were filled with mud as high as their knees... It was extremely difficult to see how the innocent children survived...children were barely surviving... " Kent sighed and shook his head. He said,

"But both children in Africa and Guatemala laugh a lot! They are more free and happier in comparison to American kids who have so much, yet are not as happy."

"Guatemala? You mean in Central America? When was that?" I have known him for a long time, and this was first time I heard about it.

"Oh, that was long time ago, between 1986 and 1987. I was there twice."

Why?

"*Well, I just wanted to help.*" He said humbly.

Many Lives Changed, Including Mine

People always see a change in me after I visit Kent. Every single time I leave his hair salon, strangers on the street never fail to come up to me and compliment me on my hair, asking, "*Who is your hair stylist?*"

"*Kent Burgess!*" I proudly announce and provide them with the location of the hair salon he owns. Oh yes, Kent is a talented hair stylist.

He is a photographer, garden designer, philosopher, father, and humanitarian. It has been my privilege to discover many facets of Kent who has enriched my life in so many ways.

The Legacy of An Artist

Abraham Mohler

Abraham Mohler is a multi-talented man who excels in art but also enjoys music and thrives on group discussions. My introduction to him came through his art.

While waiting at St. John's Mercy Hospital for the results of a health test, I walked into the courtyard to ease my mind by appreciating a magnificent work of art done by my friend, Abraham Mohler. This 10-foot by 6-foot sculpture embraces you with its depth of thought and dimension. Entitled "The Tender Way of Mercy," the art depicts the true story of Sister Catherine McAuley.

Catherine was born into a Catholic family in Dublin, Ireland, in 1778. Her father was a charitable man with a strong compassion for the poor, especially children. When Catherine was 5, her father died. Soon after, her mother died, and the McAuley children lived with an elderly, childless couple. When the couple passed away, they left a great fortune to the children.

Catherine, filled with compassion, devoted her compassion to help homeless women and children by providing homes, education, religious guidance, and health care. Catherine and her associates opened the first House of Mercy in Dublin in 1827. Several years later, Catherine founded the Sisters of Mercy, the first religious order not bound to the rules of the cloister. These Catholic sisters were free to leave the convent and walk among the poor, visiting them in their homes. The Sisters of Mercy arrived in St. Louis in 1856. In 1871, they converted a school house to a hospital and called it St. John's Hospital.

St. John's Hospital

Inside St. John's Hospital, in the open lobby, I stood in the presence of this sculpture at the hospital and thought of Catherine's story. I was moved to read a quote from her.

"This is the spirit of the order, indeed the true spirit of Mercy flowing on us."

This really moved me. Miraculously, my anxiety seemed to wash away and I was filled with inner peace. (Right) It also helped me to connect with the name of the hospital.

Newly renamed **Mercy Hospital** seemed so appropriate because I could feel the mercy flowing through me in this special environment.

What created this sense? A big part of it was the sculpture itself, a representation of mercy as though the interpretative skills of my friend, Abraham Mohler, a young and talented artist. It brought back the memory of one afternoon when I visited Abraham in his art studio as he was working on this special project. That was in 2012. He said to me,

"This is a big assignment. St. John's Mercy Hospital gave me a lot of information about Catherine McAuley. I assembled it all in my mind and then tried to compose a picture that would get to the heart of who Catherine was...

... It was her story that touched my heart. She took in women and children who were in distress. Then she bestowed her mercy on them and helped by teaching them and improving their lives." Abraham got quiet and said,

"I hope they will accept my proposal..."

An Artist's proposal

I have visited Abraham many times at his art studio. When you enter this gallery of expressions, one sees objects as Abraham interrupts them. An owl, a ballerina, a pregnant mother...for Abraham, these are more than just figures or bodies. They are expressions and mercies he has proposed and created. Admiring his stature of a dancer or a wild life creature, I asked him how he realized his vision in this form.

"I think an artist's proposal lies somewhere between the concept of the project and how the artist responds to the things he sees. First, I find it beautiful or powerful, like a baby or pregnant woman, or wildlife. I want to challenge myself to be able to create something that captures the beauty of humans or animals...but also tells a story. Like all stories, there are always aspects that are more obvious than others."

Art Studio - 1242 Gravois, St. Louis

Owl - When I walk into Abraham's art studio, a three-foot-long bronze owl creation immediately caught my attention. There are no appropriate words to describe the animalistic spirit captured by this artistic owl. I couldn't get away from his eyes. What is it about those mysterious eyes?

What was Abraham's motivation to create this realistic owl?

"Its got a powerful, mysterious, bad ass kind of animal instinct. The client wants this specific work to be on his roof, but he wants me to decide how the rest is going to look."

What is it made of?

"I sculpted the original one out of clay then molded it, which allowed me to cast the copy in different material. Mine is bronze. For me, I love to see the light and I also look for the way the light flows into the shadow."

Where does he find the "models" for his art?

"From the people in my life, from family members to interesting people. Their character and life stories are fascinating to me."

Flamenco Dancer - When I first saw his sculpture of the Flamenco Dancer at his studio, I was captivated. It was as if I was there, right in front of the dancer. So I had to ask,

"How do you choose the subjects for your art?" As usual, Abraham was in his deep thought for a while; he finally said,

"For this one, I saw the dancers first, then I wanted to recreate the feeling I got while watching them dance. Actually, there are two people that inspired me. My landlady is a dancer... she majored in dance and choreography during college... At her home, I saw pictures of her dancing...There was one photo of her in particular that was dramatic and exhilarating, and I used that image for my early sketches of the Flamenco Dancer...

... and I also have a neighbor who is in ballet. He is a Russian refugee who came here in the 90s due to persecution. He is the one introducing me to the dancing culture. He invited me to a ballet rehearsal. As I watched, I did some sketches. I was so inspired by the dancers."

Bella at Birth - Bella is Abraham's first daughter. He recreated the moment of her birth. Each time I visit his studio, I stand in front of that breathtakingly beautiful work. I look and look and absorb that "moment." (Left)

The color of alabaster stone is indescribably pure. It is a wonderfully translucent white color. It has a purity and preciousness that make it exceedingly powerful for depicting the infant. The texture is smooth, precious, and flawless. I can't find the right words to describe it. Abraham looked at this piece of art and he nodded in agreement.

"I wanted to express what my wife, Rachel, was experiencing during child birth. I wanted to experience what she went through."

The Pregnant Woman "Grace"- Birthing Center, Mercy Hospital

When he started working on this sculpture for the Birthing Center at Mercy hospital, his wife, Rachel, was pregnant. The name of this sculpture is "Grace." It illustrates the idea that two people in love come together to create a new life.

"To me, she is proud, protective, and affectionate about the baby that she is carrying. Her arms are embracing her belly -- that's powerful!" (Left)

This heart-warming pregnant mother sculpture is now displayed in the Birthing Center of Mercy Hospital.

Abraham's talent is multi-faceted. He is able to portray a wide variety of subjects and concepts as well as to be able to work with people of all ages and needs. Thus, he is able to move from creating tender mother and child sculptures to helping returning soldiers with creating sculptures about military experiences as they deal with Post Traumatic Stress Disorder (PTSD).

Navy Seal Apprenticeship

Abraham uses his art studio to teach and mentor students. He has found that the process of creation can help people heal.

In the fall of 2010, I visited his studio and noticed a young man using his hammer and chisel to work on a marble sculpture. He had been a Navy Seal stationed in Iraq and was using art to help chip away at his frequent nightmares.

Later, during our conversation in Abraham's art studio, he revealed this young artist's motivation to be at the art studio. Abraham said to me,

"He wanted to learn carving skills. As a Navy Seal, he used to be a warrior and now wants to become an artist!"

"Wow! What a remarkable transitional stage! He must have been an artist before!"

I was very impressed by looking at this Navy Seal's sculpture he was working on.

"Yes. Actually, he has been around art his whole life. His father is a sculptor and his mother is an art teacher. His interest was always in making his own art and now he is developing his own style."

Abraham paused, and there was moment of silence. With deep respect, Abraham began to share his thoughts and stories about this young artist.

"He joined the Navy just after high school and eventually made it to the rank of SEALs, the branch's special operations unit. Later, he was an instructor for the SEALs and had to deal with several of his students' deaths. He was traumatized by the tragedy of the war. Coming here to learn about craftsmanship gave this former Navy SEAL peace and is helping to keep away those bad memories."

Abraham has become his mentor and is teaching the former SEAL how to carve marble and chisel stone. Abraham paused; silence fell in between us; then, with a warm smile appeared on his face, he said,

*"I welcome anyone who is interested in creating. I get joy out of it, especially **helping veterans' rehab. This is just a bonus to me."***

Years later, while visiting his art studio, I noticed another veteran carving his stonework with his hammer. But this time, this veteran shared his experiences and opinions with me about the Vietnam War. As I was standing there between this retired soldier and another young artist, Abraham as mentor, my admiration for the true meaning of teaching and learning grew. It reminded me Confucius' saying:
* *Never be tired of learning or teaching others.*

Sundial - Missouri Botanical Garden

Standing atop a 4-foot base, a 2-foot squared sundial is located in the Ottoman Garden at the Missouri Botanical Garden. (Below) Abraham got the commission through a designer who also is an architect and is familiar with Abraham's work. As the opportunity arrived, Abraham said he jumped at the chance.

Why Sundial?

"I have always been interested in sundials because of the geometry of the lines and how they mark light and shadow, but this particular sundial is incredibly precise. It was designed by a specialist named Roger Bailey...."

Who is Roger Bailey? I wondered.

"Roger Bailey is a scientist who figured out all the mathematics behind the

lines on the sundial. He is the one who designed the lines precisely for St. Louis latitude and longitude. It keeps accurate time within 15 seconds of true solar time from now until the stone melts into the sea. He provided me with a digital file that I printed and used to etch the lines into the stone."

I was amazed!

Abraham is an exceptionally gifted artist. At the young age of 32, he has achieved the artist's dream of creating his own art work and having it displayed at public buildings, city gardens, restaurants, private homes, and art galleries.

I was wondering when he realized that this was his special talent? Was there an influential person in his life? Maybe a teacher?

And then, one day, I received an email invitation from him that unlocked the mystery.

The attachment read:

R. Brownell McGrew (Grandfather 1916 - 1994); Abraham Mohler (Grandson). „From Generation To Generation."

It was the answer to my question: undeniable evidence of his talents and natural gifts.

From Generation To Generation - OA Gallery in Kirkwood

As I walked into the art gallery, several huge oil paintings on the right side of the wall captured my attention. I was in total awe!!

The paintings were of Native Americans, with a special emphasis on the Navajo. Every one of them was impressively beautiful! It literally took my breath away. Each of Abraham's grandfather's paintings captured the emotions of these Native Americans. You could feel their lives through the depiction of their weathered and worn faces. The paintings featured detailed strokes painted with such rich color.

Personally, I have always been fascinated by Native American tribes ever since I accidentally traveled the back roads of New Mexico in the 80s. It was in the area of Taos Pueblo that I first encountered R. C. Gorman's paintings that mostly featured Navajo American Indians. I bought one of his paintings. It has been placed in the center of my bookshelf at home. As I was standing in front of Abraham's grandfather's spectacular portraits of American Indians' tribal life, I studied his art work with the blended colors and brush strokes, which gives all his paintings a photographic effect.

Grandfather - R. Brownell McGrew - The Man Who Paints the Old

The day after the art show, Abraham gave an artist's talk, which he started with a prayer.

From Abraham's memories of his grandfather, we learned that R. Brownell McGrew was a very prominent American painter in the southwest.

"My earliest memory was of being put on a horse at my grandfather's horse ranch... My very first memory about his painting was that of a Navajo Indian woman who was fixing the hair of one of her children. I remember watching grandpa working on this painting for the final touch up work. I would have been 4 years old... He died when I was 13...

... He was kind of a mysterious figure, like Santa Claus...like God, who is good to his children, but if you don't behave, you'd better watch out! He had 13 grandkids, and I was the youngest one...

... As I was growing up, I always thought I was going to be a baseball player. That's all I wanted to do, up through college at Arizona State University, received BFA in Studio Art"

Art was an easy choice for Abraham because he figured he could draw and still play baseball. So he thought if he majored in art, it would not take too much time away from baseball. One day, he drew a picture of his grandma as a gift for his father; his father looked at the picture and saw how beautiful it was. His father said to Abraham,

"If you don't pursue art, I'm going to kick your ass!" Abraham was 18 years old then.

Most artists struggle for years and years and maybe even have a second job so they can make a living. But at the age of early thirty, Abraham is a successful artist. What is the key to his success? His answer was:

"Perseverance!"

"For you, what's behind the perseverance?" I asked.

"Hope! There is hope that in the end, everything is going to work out. Behind the hope, it is faith. The faith that teaches us that God is good. There is a verse that I quote in The Bible in Matthew 6: 'Look at the birds of the air; they do not sow or reap or store away in barns, and yet your heavenly father feeds them.' Are you not much more valuable than they?"

At that moment, I was thinking what was the meaning behind the quotation when we used the word 'perseverance', it just came to me:
* **Dripping water pierces a stone; a saw made of rope cuts through wood.**

While we were growing up, our teachers and my parents frequently used this proverb when they wanted to tell us to be "perseverance", they would always say that patience and persistence can break through anything, no matter how great the difficult is.

Abraham nodded as if he was contemplating his life. Then he smiled and said,

"Before I got the assignment from Mercy Hospital, I thought that if it worked out, then this commission would get me through the year. However, I didn't know what would happen next year. I live through prayers, and the Mercy Hospital assignment just proved my prayer. Prior to that, we didn't know where the money would come from... Bang! It happened. Therefore, do not worry about tomorrow, for tomorrow will worry about itself...

... So I have faith that God will provide for us, so the hope provides us the ability to persevere through the hard times."

Hartford Coffee House - Musical Performance On Each 3rd Saturday

Abraham is always at the Hartford Coffee House to support the gathering. His support includes playing a variety of musical instruments there either alone or with a group. It always amazes me how he can use such different unique instruments. When I asked him to name all the instruments he can play, his reply was,

"I have played the banjo, guitar, and several rhythm instruments such as the Djembe, which is an African drum, Bodhran, a Celtic drum, and Limberjack, which is an Appalachian rhythm instrument."

Where did he learn all of these? I wondered.

"I took several semesters of African drumming while I was in college, and I've been playing the banjo and guitar ever since I worked at a Christian summer camp. Bodhran is an Irish drum I learned to play when I was in Scotland, studying sculpture."

Abraham's talents and leadership go beyond art to gifted discussion leader. He is able to truly "listen" to others, even those who have opposing views. He treats all people with deep respect.

Group Discussion

Abraham is not only a true artist, he is also a group discussion leader. It started out by having a group discussion at his house a couple years ago. He said,

"It was designed to get people from very different views on politics, religion, philosophy and sexuality together for a series of conversation around dinner table at my house. I figured there are very few places where that can happen in civil discourse and I wanted to give it a try. I still carry ongoing discussion with most of friends in that group..."

The interesting thing about this group is that people have totally different viewpoints about life, yet Abraham listens to the opinions in his discussion group. The topics could be abortion, gay issues, or Democrats versus Republicans. One time I invited his group for a discussion at my house. I couldn't believe how he handled the controversial topics with calmness and dignity; he was willing to listen with ultimate respect.

After the discussion was over, I asked him how he could retain that respectful attitude toward the speaker who strongly voiced views opposite from Abraham's, he said,

*"The best way to put it is that this is real human life; they have the passion to believe what they have believed in. I owe them every dignity and respect that I owe any other individual. **I try to treat each person with respect, even if I disagree with their ideas. After all, we could all hold mistaken ideas, but we are still humans with dignity and are worthy of respect.** Because I have to assume at some point that I may have a mistaken belief about something, and I would hope that somebody would be able to gently help me to see that I am not looking at it accurately....*

He stopped for a while, then he continued,

...When I am sculpting at the art studio, I listen to tapes. I once listened to a series of CDs about John Adams and Thomas Jefferson; they were friends when they worked on the Declaration of Independence. The two were like the opposite ends of rope. They were very nasty toward each other and it caused 10 years of not talking to each other until Jefferson's daughter died. John Adams's wife sent a letter to him to express their sympathy. This simple gestures -- sending letters back and forth to each other -- from tremendous friends, then vicious enemies, then the best of friends again. I thought it was very touching. So I use that as a framework. To me, my best friends may not think the way I think, but we are still friends."

For Abraham, his greatest gift is that he loves to see the light while also looking for the way the light flows into the shadow.

When he is sculpting, he strives for excellence; when he is playing music, he strives for joy; when conducting group discussion, he strives for wisdom.

As Chinese old saying:
* **Without feeling of respect, what is there to distinguish men from beasts.**
* **Wisdom, compassion, and courage are the three universally recognized moral qualities of men.**

Postscript:

In 2016, Abraham was commissioned by a business that specializes in restoring and purchasing artwork for churches in the city Brentwood, MO. It took Abraham 6 months to carve the sculpture of Mary Magdalen (Shown Left) in limestone and double size.

Formula For Success

Joe Ruzicka

When Joe Ruzicka was a student, he excelled at math. His early mathematical feats provided entry into some advanced classes. At the same time, his understanding of formulas and fast calculations provided him some added opportunities and time.

"I remember I was always sent to the hallway during math class in my elementary school years. . . . My math teacher told my parents that I was the first one to finish math assignments in the class, then I would keep bugging other kids. The teacher kept me away from other kids by sending me to the hallway for almost the entire math class."

Joe recalled those innocent days. And, I was wondering what he thought about during those free minutes out in the hallway.

The answers started coming one Sunday evening. Joe called home from Denver. He excitedly shared his newly discovered ambition - to have his own business.

"What kind of business?" His dad asked. Joe gave his dad a completely confident, without-of-a-doubt answer,

"To own a bar!"

Two years later, Joe and his two friends, Richard and Cory, who worked at the same computer company bought a bar named *Squire*. A couple years later, these three young men who were all in their early thirties opened another bar, named *Whiskey Bar* which is within walking distance from the baseball stadium, Coors Field, in one of Denver's oldest and most historic districts at the Ballpark Neighborhood.

Did they have the formula for success? We soon found out.

Whiskey Bar

The address of Whiskey Bar is 2203 Larimer Street which was named after General William Larimer who led a group of pioneers from Kansas to Denver in 1858. The building itself was once the historic Thorndyke/Burlington Hotel. It was designed back in 1890 by Frank Edbrooke, the second licensed architect in Denver. Since Joe and his friends purchased and transformed *Thorndyke Coffee House* into the **Whiskey Bar** in 2003. Since then, it has become a very popular and relaxing neighborhood bar. Who would have thought that six years later, three young computer entrepreneurs would buy another business, a restaurant named **Lobby,** two blocks from Whiskey Bar. Just like Larimer and Thorndyke, these young men are pioneering in Denver.

Among the successful business owners I personally know, Joe is probably the youngest.

Being a curious person, I have always wanted to know the secret to any successful entrepreneurship. I learned how these three young men achieved success on one of my early visits to *Whiskey Bar*. On that particular night, Joe's family and friends were celebrating his birthday. Sitting at the corner of the bar, I watched Joe comfortably mingle with different groups of his friends and regular customers. Among them were artists, real-estate agents, teachers, fashion designers, firemen, graduate students and office workers. However, one person engaged Joe in a very intense conversation. Later, Joe revealed topic of the discussion.

"Oh, that was Carlo, a philosopher. It is easy for us to discuss philosophy. . . . You know, with my mathematics background which is commonly associated with philosophy. . . . Our conversation easily led us to discussing the nature of methodology in mathematics or the place of mathematics in people's lives."

That night, I instantly formulated my first mathematic equation to describe his successful business - "gracious social skills + high intelligence = success." I presented my own theory and asked him to give me the *keys* to his successful methodology. He gave me two simple words as his answer: trust and respect.

Trust and Respect

"I didn't start the business. It was Cory and Richard. Actually, they first created their own business, called Grocery Logic which was an on-line grocery delivery business. People could order grocery items through their web site and they would go to the store to buy the food and then deliver it to the clients' homes. Their business got bigger and bigger, so they built a warehouse where there were departments for cheese, meat, bread and more. Their successful business was bought out soon... Near their warehouse, there was a corner bar, named Squire. One day, when Cory and Richard talked to the owner's wife at the bar, they found out her husband had passed away. She wanted to sell her bar, so Cory and Richard made the offer. That's how it started. . . . We were all in our twenties. . . . It sounded crazy, but we made our first simple rule: if we drank at our own bar, we paid for it. Cory is in charge of cash all day long. I don't even think twice about not trusting him. In my opinion, the key to ensuring successful team work are trust and respect. I trust and respect Cory and Richard to levels beyond belief! The three of us have worked together as a team since day one."

Team Work

"Richard and I work at the same computer company during the daytime while Cory handles all things in the Whiskey Bar. All three of us want to

succeed. *We knew from the beginning what we wanted to accomplish even though there were lots of things we didn't know, like how to get liquor license, so we learned ways to do it. We went to the library and checked out books or looked on-line to find out how to apply for a license. There were tons of things we didn't know about, but we just figured it out and followed through. It always required lots of team work. We still believe strongly that no matter what, we will work it out and totally trust and respect each other's ideas and strengths.*

Different Strengths

"Each of us has different strengths. Cory is more the "engine" type of the guy. He has the drive and desire to run business, Richard is more practical, a strategic planner. Me? I'm more the rational, sounding board for them."

These three young men have strengths that complement each other. But I wondered how these unique characteristics could be blended. They all come together because they are good friends and know how to inject fun and creativity into their blend of personalities.

"We spend fun time together. We plan 'Owners Play Day' when we clean the bar. Then, when we get done, we watch the baseball game together, or we all celebrate July 4th at the city park with our families, or we all spend the weekend at our jointly owned resort condo."

Speaking of fun times, I remember during one of my visits to Denver. As I walked in the Whiskey Bar, I immediately noticed that the Bar was packed with young adults who were focused on the TV screen, watching the presidential debate. Periodically people were cheering. I couldn't tell whether the customers were Democrats or Republicans. What puzzled me the most was that I didn't understand why they were cheering. Later, I asked Joe about this unusual political review.

"Oh yeah, at the bar that night, we set the rules for Presidential Debate Word Bingo: when the candidate used a certain word, we drank. It was

not an educational debate. It was a fun night. . . . It is not just about politics; it is about having fun together."

After Joe and his team had run the Whiskey bar successfully for years, they wanted to take on a new challenge: the restaurant business.

I decided to pay a surprise visit to the Lobby restaurant to find out the recipe for how these three good friends who were in their 30's were operating their second successful business. I walked into the Lobby purposely looking for any "sign" to the successful business. The first unusual clue to catch my eye was a frame on the wall. It listed 40 investors. Joe explained his concept:

Outside the Box

"It was my idea to ask our frequent Whiskey Bar customers to invest a relatively small amount of money into the restaurant business. It turned out that about 40 regular customers enthusiastically invested in the Lobby restaurant. Each had a portion of ownership of the restaurant. This kick-starter approach helped us achieve lots of success. We were able to sell half of the shares to the manager and his wife who now continue running Lobby beautifully."

On that special day, during the lunch, my first impression of the restaurant was that it was very casual with a pleasant atmosphere. The servers were friendly and promptly brought out delicious food. Then something unexpected caught our attention while we were tasting their famous dessert: Ice Cream Kazookie (ice cream topped with warm cookies just out of the oven), a waitress announced that there was something special about to happen. A few minutes later, the three owners followed by the main chef, came out of the restaurant, walked toward the center of the court yard. All the diners quickly stopped eating and wondered what was going to happen. First, the main chef was formally introduced to all the guests. Then, each of the three owners -- Cory, Richard and Joe -- took turns giving compliments to the chef for his major accomplishments to the Lobby, then, they presented a plaque to honor the chef for his outstanding achievement. Wow! That presentation and speech just opened up my Chinese eyes, I have never ever seen any restaurant owner(s) proudly give such recognition to the chefs in front of the customers. How smart are those three young owners, I thought! Later, after the lunch, I said to Joe,

"I know each one of you has different strengths, and the three of you guys respect and trust each other, but, from your point of view, what is the commonality among the three of you?" Again, without hesitation, Joe responded:

"*Cory and Richard are super, super, super smart!*"

Quickly, I added, "*So are you, Joe! Now the formula is: Trust and Respect + Team Work + Super, Super, Super Intelligence = Success!* " He gave a broad smile and said,

"*Well, let me be more precise about our formula for success in the restaurant business:*
* ***The desire to be a team player for our joint business: a strong focus on the strengths of each employee; a deep sense of appreciation for culinary art; a willingness to think outside the box and strong sense of finance."***

I think Joe spent time in the hallway very well!

| Whisky Bar: 2201 Larimer St., Denver, CO. (Left) | Joe and his father at the Whisky Bar (Right) |

Big Ideas, Big O

Billy Foster and Kathy Kuper

Big O is a ginger liqueur, created, developed, and sold by Billy Foster and Kathy Kuper.

When I first tasted Big O, I experienced the velvety smooth texture on my tongue, which was quickly followed by a hint of warmth as the ginger and other spices began to release and combine in perfect harmony. As a Chinese cuisine enthusiast, I knew I was going to make this new liqueur my modern Chinese cooking secret.

All Chinese cuisine feature several important basic ingredients : soy sauce, sugar, wine, and ginger. Big O contains three of these four elements (minus the soy sauce), plus brandy and other herbs and spices. Every time I add it to my seasoning sauce, it works like a charm.

I am proud to say that Billy and Kathy, a husband-and-wife team, are my good friends, and their talents have inspired me and others to create many delicious dishes and drinks with Big O.

They had never worked in the beverage industry or owned a restaurant, but that didn't stop them from developing this Missouri, home-grown business. It was their love for each other and their boundless creativity that helped them decided to market and sell this unique liqueur.

To date, they have produced 20,000 bottles and distributed them in five states : Missouri, Illinois, Delaware, Nebraska, and Louisiana. The origins of Big O came from a vacation trip to London. Billy said,

"In 2002, we took our 13-year-old son, Chris, to London," said Billy. *"One night, we ate at this Italian restaurant in Leister Square, and they served Limoncello with lemon, vodka and sugar."* Kathy added,

"It was so good served very, very cold, so I asked the waiter about the drink, and he said his grandfather made it back in Italy at home. I thought that was VERY interesting! You can make booze at home! So we tried to make limoncello, but it was terrible. We had to throw it out. Since I love ginger and ginger candy, I said to myself, 'Hmm...I wonder if we could make something like this, but with ginger? And do it ourselves?' Especially since Billy is such a good cook." But the journey from idea to success was not an easy one.

"We tried and tried and tried at home," said Kathy, *"and it was terrible! Either it was too hot or too spicy. We had tried many times, lowering or increasing or combining the ingredients in different ways for more than a year-and-a-half. But we didn't stop trying until we finally made it."*

And the Big O's secret ingredient? Fresh, organic ginger -- that's it. Nothing artificial, and everything is made by hand.

Once they came up with a recipe they were pleased with, they served their ginger liquor to their guests in their home and took it as a gift to friends' homes. One evening, I was invited by a mutual friend to a potluck party. Billy and Kathy acted as "bartenders" and served us drinks, and everyone had a chance to taste this new liqueur. The host -- our mutual friend -- is a lawyer by profession and was so impressed by the liqueur that he encouraged Billy and Kathy to trademark and sell their drink to the public.

Since that potluck dinner party, Billy, Kathy, and I have become good friends. In fact, I invited Billy and Kathy to my house for a casual gathering. As usual, I cooked Chinese food for them. I used Big O as an ingredient; I specifically made one of my favorite dishes for them, named *Lover's Shrimp*. Served on one platter, it features hot, spicy-braised prawns on one side and delicate, crystal-light prawns on the other. Both are presented on the same plate to represent a pair of lovers who might have different personalities, yet live in a harmonious relationship. This was the perfect dish for Kathy and Billy, because Kathy is direct, energetic, and strong whereas Billy is more deliberate, calm, and diplomatic. They balance each other like Yin and Yang.

Love Story

"It was the summer of 1978," said Billy. *"I was working on my Master's Degree in English Literature, and Kathy was working on her Journalism degree at the same university. I lived with several roommates in an old house that had been converted to apartments. We lived upstairs and Kathy and her friends lived downstair... It was a hot summer, and all the doors and windows were open for some air. One day, I was surprised to find a little black-and-white kitten. I scooped her up and went downstairs to see if the kitty was theirs. A really pretty girl with long blond hair came to the door, and that was it for me. I returned to my apartment and told my roommates, 'That blonde girl is mine.' Later we became great friends."*

I am so happy to be friends with this truly wonderful and loving couple. Throughout the last decade, we have gained each other's love and respect.

Family Business

It is very much a family driven business. *"We chop about 120 pounds of fresh Hawaiian ginger into small pieces,"* said Kathy. *"We add other whole spices that are not ground up or altered in any way, and a wine-based vodka and brandy. We allow the mixture to steep for at least one month. Then we remove the spices and allow the liqueur to rest for another week or so, then bottle it up....We share most jobs."* Billy nodded and said;

"*Whoever has time or is there does whatever is needed. Now Chris, our son, uses his college degree in marketing to help promote the company. He also does bottling, labeling, and chopping ginger -- just like Kathy and me.*"

In the early days, they would drive from St. Louis to Atchison, Kansas to the distillery where they would make small, 100-gallon, batches. Including travel time, the entire process took about three days before the product was ready to rest for a month, and they were back home. Kathy and Billy did this four times a year. Today they travel to a distillery in nearby St. Genevieve, Missouri. The process is still the same, but the growing business now faces the challenges of selling and promoting its product.

"*Selling our product is all about taste and building a relationship with the buyers,*" said Billy. "*We have to get people to taste it. Once they do, they love it and they will buy a bottle. Then we have to educate them about how to use Big O for making after-dinner drinks and using it as a cocktail enhancer. We have to help some bartenders recognize the potential uses of Big O and get them to begin trying it in cocktails.*"

The Big O can also stand for "Others"

There are some noteworthy differences in how they operate their business. This is how Billy explained their philosophy to me.

"*We have to be good people who make a great product and treat our clients with fairness and respect,*" he said. "*We are honest and generous and truly care about people.*" And it's true. They are the most honest, genuine, and kind business couple I've ever met.

I have seen proof of this through how they sometimes use proceeds from Big O to help others. On one occasion during a conversation, they mentioned that they were meeting up with various bartenders for a special event, "**Bar Wraps**," at the Element Lounge near downtown St. Louis. Without knowing any details, I invited myself and just showed up. There I found out that the evening's event was to raise money to help homeless children and families with housing, food, and education. I later learned that Billy and Kathy have participated in many other special events to raise funds for disadvantaged women's health services and home care for terminally ill patients and their families. These are just a few examples of what they have done to use their profits to help others.

After hearing about some of their charitable activities, there was a moment where I thought to myself, "I am in America, and for the first time I am witnessing a family create a product out of pure curiosity. And they are using some of their profits to help others -- what an inspiration! I have experienced the true meaning of the Land of Opportunity: to not only make money, but also to help people in need." If possible, I have gained an even greater admiration for this American couple.

Lessons Learned

Billy's father grew up during the Great Depression when most people lived without a lot of money or financial security. Mr. Foster worked exceptionally hard to support his family. He became a successful businessman who owned a variety of companies including pharmacies, nursing homes, hotels, and a construction company. He knew the value of working hard and success. He also believed that his children should strive for financial success.

As he was growing up, Billy found himself questioning this reasoning. Should you base the value of a person on how much money they make or how big their wallet is? He believed there was more to it. Billy went on to college where he pursued several majors and finally settled on an English degree, much to his father's dismay. Billy went on to work as an English professor and taught many writing courses and later worked as an administrator and assistant professor at The University of Missouri in St. Louis. He retired early and began his own business, which resulted in Big O.

Ironically, it was after he retired from his teaching profession that he became a successful businessman. Billy - with Kathy and Chris - works hard and provides job opportunities for others, just as his father had wished. I learned that Billy's father, before he passed away in 2014, was very proud of him.

Teacher in China

Billy gained my instant respect when I learned about his role as a teacher in China. In the spring of 2003, the Dean of English Education at UMSL asked Billy to prepare college student teachers for international teaching assignments by traveling with them to China to help them adjust to the culture and lifestyle. They began with three days in Beijing before traveling to Fuxin. He began by making sure the teachers' accommodations were in good order. He recalled his responsibility during those years:

"I helped college students navigate the labyrinth of things they had to do before they could begin teaching...I also had to negotiate the teachers' assignments, duties, and compensation with the school leadership and local government officials. I took between five and twelve student teachers each trip." In all, he traveled to China seven times.

Teachers in China have the highest levels of public respect. They are compared with doctors and engineers who are highly trusted and admired.

Billy not only taught American college students, but also advised culinary students on how to be successful chefs in America. L'Ecole Culinaire in St. Louis asked Billy to become a member of its Program Advisory Committee because of his extensive educational background. He gave the commencement address for the graduating class of 2015. In his speech, he talked about his own experience learning to cook. He based his speech on things he has learned in life, but the upshot was to always be optimistic, flexible and kind. When I asked him what would be his personal belief behind the speech, he said;

Be the person who looks into a pantry and sees a feast where others see nothing to eat.

Billy's teaching career is best exemplified by the saying of Confucius:
* *Teaching without thinking is useless, but thinking without education is more dangerous!*

Billy Foster and Kathy Kuper

Big O

Lost and Found

Mark Lee

One day, an email appeared on my computer in my school office. It read:

… Hi, Mrs. Liu. This is Mark Lee. Do you remember me? I found out that you are at Alternative Discipline Center now. I wanted you to know that you had a huge positive impact on my life. You made me believe in myself. I graduated from college and I am now a General Manager for a national company in Texas. I am married and have two boys. I hope you remember me and write me back soon. Mark Lee, Class of 1987….

I was in shock -- and extremely humbled. Of course I remembered Mark – a very polite and popular student at Parkway South High. His email brought back memories. He was clean cut, good looking, never in trouble, and very involved with high school sports. I wondered about his life and how he "found" me after twenty years. His second email arrived shortly after I responded.

… I searched you through Google on the school web site and found your name in the staff directory. Mrs. Liu, BECAUSE OF YOU, I am what I am. Thanks for always believing in me… If I can ever help with any of your students, please let me know. I will be calling you soon as well…"

During our first phone call, he explained why he went looking for me after all this time.

...I have been looking for you, Mrs. Liu...I am so glad I finally found you... high school is a difficult time for any teenager...At that time in my life, in my mind, I always knew that you were there, even though you might not be in the same room at the time, but I always knew where you were...I knew I could talk with you...In my life during high school, sometimes I said to myself 'Ok...go ahead and try it, and even if you fail, you've got Mrs. Liu there to help you...

I couldn't believe it! It didn't seem like Mark needed any extra help from me, except for maybe with math once in a while. He didn't seem to have any problems and had many friends at school. He explained:

...Even though I had friends at school, my life was not constant. YOU were constant throughout my high school years..."

Well then, I must have had an easy teaching job. Whenever he needed to talk at school, he could find me in my room.

Now, after exchanging emails and phone calls, Mark told me more about his adult life.

Mark graduated from Southeast Missouri State, majoring in mass communications/ public relations, with a minor in organizational communications. He landed a job as the senior event coordinator at a brand new concert arena in Moline, Illinois. Years later, he hired and trained all the event staff and worked with some really big-name concert promoters.

Then he took his father's advice and moved to Dallas where he started as a sales person and worked his way up to director of sales at a company named The Expo Group, which specialized in the management of large national and state professional associations.

His families still reside in Missouri. They return to visit for holidays or family events. After we reconnected, my place also became "a stop" on Mark's visits to Missouri from Texas. He brings his two sons,

Johnson Thomas (who likes to be called J.T.) and Benjamin. I always welcome them.

During our first few visits, Mark continued to say that it was me who helped him through his teenage years. I seriously doubted it. I simply did not remember him as a troubled teenager who needed anything special from me. So my teacher's instinct kicked in and I told myself that there was something more to it than that. I started asking him how his teenaged mind worked during those high school years.

Imaginary Classroom

"I think I could tell if teachers were trying to really make a connection between the students and the subject. I feel Mr. Wade did this... For example, as a senior in algebra, I could always understand the mathematical process, but made lazy mistakes...

...My mind ran too fast. There was a constant battle to fight boredom in my brain, so Mr. Wade challenged me and never treated me like a kid who was behind. He allowed me to teach basic concepts to his pre-algebra class. I always reverted back to that style of learning, especially later in college... If I needed to learn something, I mean really learn it, I would pretend that there was an imaginary classroom full of students and I would 'teach' them, and even pose questions to myself as though the imaginary students were asking...then, I realized that I had a unique way of learning."

Did he use his "imaginary classroom" skills during college?

"I consider myself very hyper because my mind is constantly stimulated. During my college days, I heard in one of my college classes that frequent starts and stops while studying would actually make you learn the subject even better. I realized my brain could easily recall what it was I was studying, whenever I first started, and then again right before I would take a break. Therefore, by moving those starting and stopping episodes closer together, the better my memory recall."

Mark had created his own study method! It helped create his path to academic success in his college years. I wanted to know more about how his mind worked in that particular way. He said;

"I got it from my grandparents. They lived in a small town...I learned that either you have to speak up or step down...

... I also learned from my grandparents that you had to let your personality shine..."

Shine Like the Morning Sun

Yes, I remember seeing Mark Lee throughout high school, and his personality did shine like the morning sun, whether he was in the classroom, walking in the hallway, playing tennis, or taking pictures for the yearbook. He was always confident, engaging, smiling, accepting, cooperative, and respectful. How did he learn this from his family?

"Living in a small town with my grandparents, they would be into so many things like church functions, family relations...sometimes, my grandparents would take me down to visit their high school friends, or relatives from old farms when we had nothing else to do. We could go outside on the grass, but there was nothing to do, so I had to come out of that by using every stimulation to bring myself out of that setting...talked to different kinds of people...learned to connect with them...

... It is amazing that by spending time with my grandparents while growing up, I just overcame and learned to entertain myself, talked to different kinds of people...I learned a lot..."

I, too, learned a lot about Mark when he visited me. When he was in high school, he was very easy-going, whether in class or out. Mark was not shy nor overbearing. If there was a social skills class, he would have earned an A+. He must have read my mind. He continued;

"I spent lots of time with my mom, sister, and grandmas on both sides. I have confidence with girls and women. All those women are so different from each other. I learned how to treat women..."

Now I understand why he is so successful in what he does as the regional director of sales for an audio/video presentation company that helps to stage corporate events. Whether in the classroom or with different kinds of people or situations, Mark Lee adapted and learned from them.

Chameleon

"I am a chameleon, with a little technology!" His answer gave me more insight.

"But!" He smiled and continued, *"Without losing myself! I walk into an environment or meeting with different people, and I can be a chameleon, but still be myself...I can change my personality or words to determine what they want and gain their trust..."*

Since we reconnected more than ten years ago, I've watched his two sons grow from preteens to young adults. Now, J. T. is in college.

As the Chinese proverb goes: ***Time flies like an arrow!*** Last time he stayed with me, I noticed that he closed the door after he and his sons finished watching a movie. The following day, he shared with me the nature of their father-son discussion.

"Last night, I spoke to my sons about the theme of the movie: how we deal with different and/or difficult personalities. This time it was about gay issues because of the movie. My advice for them is just to remember that everyone is different, be open minded, don't be judgmental...I told my sons my view toward the gay issue, that it doesn't bother me at all. It is not my lifestyle, but I don't need to be judgmental about other people's..."

J.T. admires his father. He is following Mark's footsteps by attending Southeast Missouri State and even became a member of the same fraternity.

"I have realized that Jonathan needs to figure out his path on his own and not go down the path I have made for him. Don't chase my dream, I said to him; rather chase your own dream."

Mark's advice to his oldest son brought back a memory about my oldest brother, Foch, who shared a story with me while visiting me from California a few years ago. Foch noticed a large photo hung in my living room. It was a scene of a monk in contemplation looking at the desert. My brother took that picture when he was traveling in Tibet. That caused Foch to reflect. Then, he shared a story with me from the time when he was a teenager.

"Our father came to my room one evening in my senior year and asked me what I wanted to study in college. My answer was either art or literature. Father didn't say a word and walked out of my room. A few minutes later, mom came in and told me that our father was very disappointed in me because I did not consider my younger siblings. Since I am the oldest one, taking care of the younger ones was my major responsibility. Therefore, I needed to rethink my future plan and become either an engineer or scientist in order to support the younger brothers and sisters...

What amazed me was what my brother said after telling me the story.

...Actually, it worked out pretty well. Because of my PhD in physics, I had a good career. Since I have retired, I have traveled all over the world, and photography and writing have become my passion. Now, you see, you have my artwork in your house!"

So the lesson was that my brother's job provided the security for the family and enough monetary support to follow his dream when his career was over.

When Mark expressed to me that he wanted his son, J. T., to not follow in his footsteps, but rather, to pursue his own dream, I realized there is a huge difference in parental advice between the Chinese tradition and the American culture.

What fatherly advice would Mark give his sons other than pursue their own dreams?

This is what an American father, my former student Mark said to me:

Fatherly Advice:

* *Make a difference in someone else's life.*
* *It is okay to question authority, but with respect*
* *Don't let your age define you.*
* *Love of learning is the greatest thing in life.*
* *Truth is really what you should be seeking.*
* *If you are going to learn in this life, you have to be okay with pain that may come with that wisdom.*

Mark Lee and I had **LOST** contact after he graduated from high school. I was humbled that he was determined to find me. After we reconnected, I, his high school teacher happily **FOUND** insightful, intuitive, perceptive wisdom in his learning style, career foundation and parental skills that are admirable beyond belief. It is another example of the American way -- teachers learning from their students.

Famous Chinese proverbs about father and sons:
* *A filial son makes a father rest easy.*
* *Wise father, loving son.*

Confucius :
* *The father who does not teach his son his duties is equally guilt with the son who neglects them.*

Postscript:

Mark Lee followed through on the promise made during our first phone call. He visited my classroom and participated in a discussion with my students about what needs to be learned in high school, pursuing higher education, and how to face life's challenges. It was a joy to watch the student become the teacher.

(Left to right: Mark Lee, J. T., Benjamin)

The Making of a Young Egyptologist

Katherine Dowling

The first time I met Katherine, her mother had brought her to the learning center where I worked, I asked Katherine why she was there, and she told me she didn't like 5th grade math, but she **loved** to read.

Within five minutes of meeting her, Katherine's independent thinking and no-nonsense personality were front and center.

I told her that there were many ways to learn math, and she looked surprised. I suggested that each time we met, I would introduce her to a new math concept or skill, and she would tell me about the books that she had read that week. She willingly accepted my offer.

I didn't know at the time that it was the beginning of a years-long friendship with this fantastic young girl who would grow into a strong, smart, beautiful woman before my eyes.

Private vs. Public High School

Katherine's education started in a private school, but with declining grades, she moved to public school in the ninth grade. We continued to work together on math -- and share stories with each other about our lives.

Her mother would drop her off at a Starbuck's Coffee House where we met on Saturdays at the end of each semester. Then, when she got her driver's license her junior year in high school, she would drive there herself. I always got myself coffee and hot chocolate for her. Now she is entering her junior year in college.

During her first year at public school, our topics drastically changed. Instead of discussing academic subjects, she expressed her impression of public high school. I was fascinated for a couple of reasons: I attended a public school while growing up in Taiwan and had been an American public high school teacher my entire career.

In Her Own Words

"The change from private school to public school was scary at the beginning. You feel small and there are more people, taller, stronger than you... more different kinds of kids. Some may wear pajamas or wear head bands to school... it doesn't matter...

... First, I didn't tell anyone that I was from private school, but, once they found out, they said, 'Okay,' then I was more relaxed. Nobody judges you, there are no confrontations, no one watches you 24/7... they tend to accept you...

... The downside about public school is drugs. Drugs are a big problem...

... I always said NO! to them cause I don't do that...if I started it, then it will go downhill pretty soon. I have no desire...besides you don't know what is in it...My dad said so...."

I looked at her and asked,

"Is your dad a teacher or counselor?"

"He is a brain surgeon... Another reason I don't accept it is I already struggled with my money. Buying drugs is a waste of money... I have to work at it...

... ironing my dad's clothes is my job. It is an indoor job, not an outdoor job, and I get one dollar for one item. On average, I get paid $14 a week...I use the money to buy chocolate ice cream and Kindle books...I love to read, so I use most of my money to buy books... though I do save my money...

... I read about 10 books a week."

Shadowing Program

Katherine's father works at Washington University as a brain surgeon. She once shadowed her father at work by participating in the Shadowing Program. It makes me admire her -- and her parents -- even more.

"The first case I was watching that day, they used some kind of machine. It made me nauseous, so I had to sit down, then I went to another room... we were there for two hours. I just watched this big screen and saw how my dad operated on his patient's brain. It was a dark room, big TV... my dad had to remove something in his patient's brain."

"What did you learn from shadowing your dad?"

"I learned that dad does really work hard. He is on his feet constantly... So when my younger brothers say, 'Why is dad not home yet?,' I can just say, 'You know what? Dad works hard to save people's lives.' That is what they need to be concerned about."

Beauty Pageant

I was invited to attend Katherine's second beauty pageant during her high school senior year. There were six girls in the competition that day. With her beautiful and warm smile, Katherine walked confidently onto the stage. I was extremely proud of her.

I held back my tears and thought, '*That is a girl who is confident and has great self esteem. That is true beauty!*' She doesn't use makeup because she is naturally a beautiful girl. She didn't win the title, but to me, she was the most beautiful girl there.

Later that weekend at Starbucks, she proved me "right" when she said;

"*I knew I was not going to win, but I had fun. I did it last year when there were 12 girls in competition. I didn't win beauty last year, but I won the Best Character... I had fun ...It is not about winning. I just wanted to get together with a bunch of friends and enter a dance contest together with them.*"

"*This time you did a dance routine with other competitors. What did you do last time?*"

"*Last time, I did fencing!*"

To me, she is a true beauty, inside and out.

After-School Extra Activities

With her parents' encouragement, Katherine did volunteer work during her senior year. I remember the Saturday morning we met in February at Starbucks. As usual, she was excited as she brought me up to speed on her life.

"*I have been volunteering at Children's Hospital to care for children with cerebral palsy for a few weeks through Camp Independence. The camp helps kids do activities they normally wouldn't get a chance to do, like play tennis and swim. They look like every other kid. Every morning we would help them to stretch, and then have them walk around the gym... Also, I did volunteer work for Habitat for Humanity.*"

"*You've got great parents! That's wonderful you do volunteer work to help others. Did you do any paid job?*"

"I have worked at YMCA as a swimming instructor. I taught one little girl to swim. I said to her, 'You need to strengthen your skills.' I am so happy to see her improvement. She now can swim on her own. That job did pay about $ 8.00 an hour, which isn't much, but when you rack up 20 hours a week, it turns into a nice paycheck. I use the money to buy books."

Among all the extra school activities Katherine was involved with over the summer, Outward Bound had the biggest impact on her.

Outward Bound

Outward Bound is an international, nonprofit, independent, outdoor educational organization with about 40 schools around the world. The Outward Bound program in which Katherine participated was in the Appalachian Mountains in North Carolina. Her mother encouraged her to attend the two-week program.

"My mom wanted me to join the Outward Bound program. She wanted me to learn discipline, as well as see what it's like for two weeks out in the woods on our own, without a lot of food. I did whitewater canoeing for three days and hiked about five miles each day. There were three girls and nine boys in the program that I attended. The purpose is to build responsibility and character, and to think about life in a different way."

*"What did **you** learn from the program?"*

"I learned that I was stronger than I thought. At the end of a seven-mile run, which took me 2-1/2 hours to finish, I was exhausted. My friends kept saying 'Come on, let's go, let's have a drink, let's eat!' But I kept thinking that even though I was the last one, I completed it! I finished it! That was important."

Last Muddy Mile

Like many senior year high school students, Katherine worked at applying for college admission. Among all the applications she sent out, four colleges accepted her. She believed her essay, titled *Last Muddy Mile*, was the key factor for the college acceptances. She explained,

"I named it Last Muddy Mile based on the experience I had at Outward Bound and how it changed my perspective on everything... took me a long time to do that essay... I am so happy I got accepted because all my hard work paid off."

*"What is **your** main point in the essay?"*

*"**There are bumps in the road... you have to get yourself up**..."*
"How did you just keep going?"

"I think the main thing is like the song 'Once Upon a December.' I kept singing it in my head. I have an i-phone that I used to listen to it over and over. It goes like this:

> Dancing bears, painted wings
> Things I almost remember
> And a song someone sings
>
> Once upon a December
> Someone holds me safe and warm
> Horses prance through a silver storm
> Figures dancing gracefully across my memory

"You gained self confidence! " I complimented her.

"Oh yeah! In this seven-mile run at Outward Bound, I was the last one... it was a rainy day...I was proud of myself, even though I was the last one to finish. But you know what? I did it. Because of my experience, I can tell people and say, 'Now you tell me you can't do this'"

While applying for colleges, she experienced some bumps in the road. After listening to her frustration, occasionally I would provide some indirect advice through my questions like a teacher would do. But for the most part, she gained her own wisdom through her own experiences. I praised her for her down-to-earth insightfulness, especially at the young age of 18. She said:

"I am applying to colleges that have Egyptology, like Harvard, Brown University...but, they all need 4.0 students. So what I told them was that even though my grades were not good during freshmen and sophomore years, look at me now -- from Ds and Cs to As and Bs. Some people may have good grades, but in real life, they are dumb as door nails. They may think of me and say 'Hmm, she has something to offer,' instead of judging me by my grades..."

"Is there any advice you would give to senior high school girls?"

*"When I went to parties with my friends, I always put my finger in the top of my soda bottles to make sure that no one would slip anything in my drink. It may have looked weird, but it was smart on my part. Basically, be careful who you trust. **Choose your friends wisely, and remember, your true friends are the ones who stick with you through tough times** - as well as always keep your drink in your sight."*

"Any other advice?"

"If you are friends with your high school principal, you know the principal will protect you. I know my principal well. So the next college I apply to, I want my principal to write a recommendation letter for me."

How did she start to show interest in becoming an Egyptologist? I wondered.

The Road to Becoming an Egyptologist

"I took French from 3rd to 5th grade at my primary school. I took world history in high school and now I am taking anthropology class in college...

... I even went to a museum in Chicago to see King Tut when I was in 5th grade. That's when I got interested in it."

"What? You saw King Tut in Chicago?"

"Yeah! That's how I started to like King Tut. When I was in the 5th grade, we were studying King Tut. My mom knew that I was interested in learning more, so we all took a trip to Chicago. My twin sister Caroline and my younger brothers were like 'Oh no, this is so boring.' To me, it was so cool."

"Which part of that trip interested you the most?"

"I found out that these things were thousands of years old. They were preserved so well, and the Egyptians knew how to take care of them so well. They looked like they were just made yesterday. It was totally a shock to me -- those masks were so shiny and they were still standing."

"You like old stuff. No wonder you like me!" I made the comment.

"Yea, I DO love old stuff... and old buildings like my school. I purposely chose to stay in the oldest dorm (oldest structure). The window has so many leaks, it's freaking freezing cold in winter, but I don't want to change. When my friends come to my room, they say, 'Wow, your room is so interesting!' ... I have three bookshelves which are mostly filled with books about Egypt. My own bed at home is the oldest one in the house. Everything in my room has history...

... I know I have lots of years to study. I know I may not even get a job because of my major and I may be in my 30s when I finish all my studies. But I still want to do it. I feel very passionate about that."

"What do your parents or school advisor think about this?"

"My mom says I need to study a major that will help me find a career so that I can make a living. But, you know what? This is the one thing that I am passionate about. My advisor asked me whether I have changed my major for next year. I said NOPE, I still want to major in Egyptology; she was impressed. She said lots of freshmen didn't know what to major in or change majors many times by now. But not me."

"What about your friends?"

*"They all said 'NO.' They said, 'You will stick out like a sore thumb in Egypt,' because I look too pale. I said, you know what? '**Not everybody is who he or she appears to be on the outside!"***

From 5th Grade Math Tutor to Friend

Sitting by the window at Starbucks, looking outside at the parking lot, cars came and went. I realized Katherine and I have been sitting in the same chairs almost 10 years. She has just finished her sophomore year at Missouri State University.

Because of her, I've studied more about King Tut and Tut's discoverer, the British scientist, Howard Carter. As Carter entered the tomb, he was staggered with every step. The recounted stories are spine-tingling and reflect the awe of the discovery. When asked, *"Can you see anything?"*

"Yes, wonderful things." Carter responded.

When I reflect on Katherine, I, too, see wonderful things. And I feel confident she will continue to grow and fulfill her dreams. Our  friendship also continues, text each other regularly. I expect one day to hear about her adventures in Egypt and it wouldn't surprise me if she even writes a book about it to add to her bookshelf. Last time we met the coffee house,(Left) as usual. But, instead of asking her same questions: what books she had read and what goal in her next semester, I gave her two Chinese proverbs:

* ***A wise man makes his own decisions, an ignorant man follows the public opinion.***
* ***A good book is a good friend.***

Fun: Wheeled American Style!

Mandy Ruzicka

Mandy lives a fun life, full of extraordinary activities and incredible adventure.

It's a journey to hear everything she has accomplished. She has climbed rock walls, has sung at the White House, met celebrities, has swum with dolphins, and has competed in races to raise money for charities. Most recently she published her first book, **Fun: Wheeled American Style.** (Below)

She is an exceptional person with tremendous gifts and she has done it all in a wheelchair!

"I have lived this way...and written about it in my book because I want to show that people in wheelchairs really can have a lot of fun. And that we, too, live 'normal' lives. After all, there shouldn't be an ability level on fun, right?"

I was impressed by her positive attitude. Through our conversations, I gained even more admiration for her openness. Among all the things she has done, I wanted to learn about rock climbing first.

How did she do it?

Climbing the Rock Wall

"First, I was strapped into a harness while sitting in my wheelchair. Then, using a rope pulley, I was lifted up in the seating position...then was picked up and put on the wall, kind of like a fly. Then, I was told to climb to the nearest rock, so I pulled myself up to the first rock...then the next one...then the next one..."

"Were you scared? How did you feel?" I asked.

"I felt great, but kind of scared at the same time. During the whole time climbing, I kept telling myself, 'Mandy, you can do it. Great job!' Just like my father always said to me - Great job!"

Mandy stopped and looked at me. She asked,

"Do you remember the part in Finding Nemo when Dora was singing 'Just keep swimming, swimming, swimming!...' Well! I was singing that song in my head at that time, but instead, I...used the word, climbing, climbing, climbing...All of a sudden, I looked up and I realized I had made it to the top...I said to myself, 'Oh my gosh! That's high! Yay! I made it to the top!'...It felt wonderful!"

Visiting the White House

When she was little, Mandy belonged to an organization in St. Louis called *"Variety the Children's Charity of St. Louis."* This charity buys medical equipment and provides positive and fun activities for children with physical and developmental disabilities in and around the St. Louis area. Mandy was their poster child when she was only two years old.

"The members have helped me tremendously! In 2003, when I was in my senior year in high school...somehow, I got invited to the White House!"

"White House? What did you do? Did you see the President? What was it like in the White House?" I asked.

Mandy is the first person I've known who has been invited to the White House. I wanted to know more.

"George W. Bush was President at the time. We were asked to sing as part of a Christmas choir...I remember there was this huge, gigantic Christmas tree in the Blue Room! I had never seen anything like that! I was told later that all of the ornaments were first used by Barbara Bush in 1989! Also, that particular tree was grown in Wisconsin... it was so cool! That day, there were lots of tourists who listened to us sing, and then people took some pictures or talked to us afterwards. But we didn't get to see President Bush that day... But, we did see President Bush's dog; his name was Barney, a black Scottish Terrier. He was so cute, so cute!"

Kissing the Dolphins

In 2009, Mandy's whole family - including her parents and her sister, Angela - went to Sea World in Orlando. Even though she had gone on a lot of fun vacations, this one really stood out. The best part was when she swam with dolphins.

"My parents rented a beach wheelchair for me so I could swim! I had not done it before. At first, it was scary, but my dad pushed me into the water and said, 'You can do it'... the waves were splashing all around me...one even knocked me out of my chair...the water was really cold; I remember that I was wearing a life jacket and was really afraid, but very excited. Before I got into the water, I thought I might drown. My dad was with me, holding me up by my waist from behind...I was really scared...I even got the chance to kiss the dolphin, it felt rubbery, slippery and cold...It was tough using a wheelchair in the water...but, it was worth it... I am glad I got the chance to experience it... it was so much fun...my dad always encourages me to try new things, not to be afraid, just to try it."

Racing for the Charities

Racing? How and where?

"I did it because my mom's friend has a granddaughter with a congenital heart defect. It was volunteer work for this charity called CHD (Congenital Heart Defect). All the people who wanted to help raise money for this charity came to race on the trail, around Muny Park. I was the only one who joined them by sitting in a wheelchair...it was fun! Really fun!"

Mandy's volunteer work does not stop there. After five years of racing for charities, she has used her time to embroider, crochet, knit, or make ceramic plates to sell for the charities. Frequently, she asks friends if there is anything that she can make for them!

"Once in a while, I sell to friends so I can use the money to help pay for family vacations, but most of time I would just give things away. If I am not making any thing, I read. Right now I am reading Christopher Paul Colfer's book, you know the actor who is in the TV show, Glee, I am a huge fan of his. Actually, I met him in person. That was real fun!"

Meeting Celebrities

When she was only 2 years old, Mandy met Sammy Davis, Jr., even though she doesn't really remember the experience. She has also met Kurt Warner, former quarterback for the St. Louis Rams, and Donny Osmond.

"I saw Donny a couple of times. He is very nice. The first time we met, he said, 'Hi, I am Donny!' He reached out, wanting to shake my hand. I said, 'But, I need a hug.' So he gave me a big hug. That was very nice of him. Then, I pointed to my ear and showed him my new earring and said to Donny 'I just got my ears pierced today.' He said, 'Oh cool!'"

Mandy gave me a huge smile.

*"I am really a huge fan of Christopher Paul Colfer. He plays the character, Kurt Hummel on **Glee**. I met him in 2011, when he was turning 21. Because I was such a huge fan, I wanted to give him something special. So, I made a large ceramic plate to present to him when my parents brought me to Indianapolis to watch the live show....*

*...That night, I gave a plate to his bodyguard and told him that I had made it especially for Chris' birthday. Later, his bodyguard came back and said that Chris would come out and meet us...He did, and we took pictures with him. He has published a series of books called **The Land of Stories**. I have read them all...like **Wishing Spell**, which was number one on The New York Times Best Seller list."*

The ceramic plate she designed for Chris was in a large, circular shape with the word "*Glee*" painted black at the bottom of the plate. Musical notes were all around the plate, and she painted the words "*blue slushy*" also in black.

"What? Blue slushy?" I asked.

*"It replicates the blue slushy that was thrown in Chris' character's face by the jocks on **Glee**. On this particular show, they sang the New Directions' song, 'Loser Like Me.' The song is about people who may have been bullied and treated like outcasts, and how they can use these experiences to rise above the real losers. The band's performance ends with New Directions throwing confetti slushes at the audience, an imitation of how they are often slushed..."*

I asked if she had ever experienced anything like that. Mandy was very candid and willingly shared her experience.

"My physical condition is called spina bifida. It is a birth defect. It all relates to your brain and spinal cord not being properly attached. This causes the collection of lots of water in the brain. They have to put a shunt in the brain that allows water or fluids to move from one part of the body to another...or absorb all the water. Sometimes, it causes learning disabilities... it makes me discouraged when I think about it."

During my teaching career, I had to deal with bullying behavior among students occasionally. Considering Mandy's physical condition, I wondered about her experience. She said,

"Oh yes! It was in the restroom when I was in fourth grade; I was ten years old. I was ready to wash my hands. I remember this girl acting as though she wanted to beat me up because I asked her to move. She flipped out...well, I didn't realize she took my request offensively. I did report it to the school... that girl was eventually expelled because of her violent behaviors toward other students."

How did her parents react? Would any parent react differently?

"My dad did speak up and confronted the authorities." Mandy gave me a big smile and said,

"I am proud of both of my parents and how they talk about this sensitive issue openly, and give people awareness of how to treat people like us...my mom and dad have wanted people to treat me with respect all my life."

Falling Down

What I admire the most about Mandy is her attitude about life. Her stories always end with words like:

"It was fun...It was worth it...I am glad I did it..."

I wanted to know what was the secret to her happiness.

Her answer was that she was grateful for many things in life and always counted her blessings. A few years ago, she had a scary accident that actually helped her gain more of an appreciation for those blessings.

Mandy had a really bad accident. She fell down the stairs in her wheel chair and was in a coma for six days. When she finally regained consciousness, she recovered. She found encouragement from her parents. Her father inspired her to count her blessings.

"My dad is a pretty strong father. After the accident, he and I had a heart-to-heart talk. I remember he said to me, 'You know, there is a famous proverb, only two words. **"Accidents happen!"** **Accidents happen to anyone! You just get back up when accidents happen.**"

A big warm smile reappeared on her face, she continued:

"Sure enough, I did get back up. I used to be able to transfer myself from the bed and into the wheelchair. After the accident, I couldn't do it for a while because I had lost some confidence. I needed somebody to pick me up from bed and put me back in the wheelchair. That was the most terrible feeling in the world. But, it was my dad's, my mom's and my sister's constant encouragement that helped me to regain my confidence and get back to normal....

Mandy gave me this huge smile and continued her final thought.

...Most importantly, I learned to count my blessings."

Counting Her Blessings

Since the accident, Mandy's attitude has been even more optimistic and positive about life. The fall gave her the biggest life lesson: Count your blessings! And, since the accident, Mandy's attitude has been even more optimistic and positive about life. The fall gave her the biggest life lesson: **Count your blessings and be grateful every day.**

Sitting in her wheelchair, she said to me,

"I am grateful for my sense of humor, patience, and ability to communicate with people. All of these [attributes] help me understand people better."

I am a huge fan of Mandy's, the great author of _**Fun: Wheeled American Style!**_ Never have I met such a courageous and loving person. Mandy is able to rise above her disability and all the challenges that come her way because of a positive attitude that helps her to wheel her way through life.

As Chinese proverbs stated:
* _**The greatest glory is not in never falling, but in rising every time you fall.**_
* _**If you survived a storm, you won't be bothered by the rain.**_

Love on Top

Tauriana Lyles King

Every summer on Wednesday night, Steve and I pack our simple picnic and go to the Missouri Botanical Garden to enjoy the free concert. We appreciate the beauty of the Garden grounds and all the seasonal blooms in the summertime as we listen to the grooves and rhythms of an electric rotation of artists from week to week. This particular Wednesday evening, we walked around the crowded ground to look for an empty spot. As we were approaching the right side of the stage, a couple smiled at us, pointing to the open space next to their seats. We took the offer which turned out to be the perfect spot! It was closer to the stage, and behind the stage was an easy way out when the concert is over. Eli and Tauriana introduced themselves to us and quickly offered their food and drinks to us. We talked, laughed, ate, drank... All four of us had a great time while listening to the band playing Motown music. Since that night, we have met them almost every Wednesday to enjoy this open-air festival free evening concerts under the stars from June to August. We have also grown to become like a family. Both Eli and Tauriana began calling me, "Mama Liu," a nickname only my closest family and younger friends use. I thought to myself, without any legal documentation or signature, I just adopted a son and daughter. Coincidentally, Tauriana and my only daughter, Helen, share some fundamental strengths: highly intelligent and very independent.

Missouri Botanical Garden

We met them every Wednesday for music at the Garden during summer time. In addition to deepening our friendship, the time spent together gave me a chance to learn more about the Missouri Botanical Garden from Tauriana and the reason why she supports the Garden. During one of our conversations, Tauriana said,

"These free concerts are funded by the Whitaker Foundation which supports St. Louis arts and parks to promote common heritage, celebrate diversity, and encourage vitality within the community. Besides, we love music and the beautiful flowers we see in the Garden all year round! "

Tauriana's appreciation for the *Missouri Botanical Garden* reminded me of a quote from the Belgian playwright and poet, Maurice Maeterlinck, who said,

"Can we conceive what humanity would be if it did not know the flowers?"

As time passed, we also became very aware that the bond between us was growing, meshed together beautifully across multi-cultural, racial, and generational gaps.

The following year, Steve and I were invited to their wedding as friends of honor. Their wedding stands out as very distinct and memorable to me. The wedding of Tauriana and Eli mixed customs from long ago with symbolism significantly their own. Everything about this event was meaningful for me as I learned to appreciate different cultures and values.

Wedding Planning

The location, guest list, songs, dance, reception... everything was chosen with specific attention to detail. This was not a cookie-cutter wedding; it was a very special event designed for very special people who embraced tradition and symbolism. It all started with the selection of a location. Tauriana recalled,

"I had three choices for my wedding: My first choice was the Old Court House in downtown St. Louis for historical reasons; second was the Botanical Garden for the beauty and the final choice was the Jewel Box in the Forest Park."

Old Court House

"The Old Court House is just two-blocks from the Gateway Arch. It has a strong historical value. In addition, the building features a circular shape. I loved the idea of having a wedding where all the people encircle you, sharing the moments together. I wanted everybody to feel a part of the wedding because my idea was that we were surrounded by the love of our friends..." Tauriana paused, then continued:

"...But, there is also some painful history associated with the Old Courthouse. Eli was not sold on this site because all he could see was the slavery side. Outside the Courthouse was where the slaves were sold. Even now, there is a statue about slavery right in front of the building. Eli could not accept the idea of having our wedding at the Old Court House."

As the debate over the wedding site continued, Tauriana's reasoning regarding the choice of this site motivated me to do my own research on the Old Courthouse. I found out that the St. Louis Courthouse was the location of the famed Dred Scott case in 1857. A slave sought freedom for himself and his family. The case was unsuccessful. However, the judge called for a retrial. Dred Scott was a slave and at that time was considered property. His "owner" had died and the property was transferred to a family member who lived in New York, a "free state." The case was appealed, then, re-appealed, and ultimately reached the Supreme Court that ruled against Scott. The case also helped raise tensions in the United States leading to the Civil War.

Even though the St.Louis Old Courthouse has undeniably significant historical and architectural meaning, Tauriana decided not to have the wedding there. Her reason was more personal and symbolic.

"At the time we were planning our wedding, the Old Courthouse was using a government grant to renovate their space, and it was not going to be finished by the time of our wedding. With all of that scaffolding, it looked like the entire courthouse had braces."

After thoughtful discussions of possible pros and cons for other two choices, both Tauriana and Eli reached a final decision and joyful mutual agreement: The Jewel Box in Forest Park would be the location of their wedding.

Jewel Box in the Forest Park

Whenever I have out-of-town guests, the Jewel Box in Forest Park is on my must-see list. Built in 1936, it is an artistic floral conservatory. It has been listed in the National Registry of Historic Places. I always brag about it for its radical engineering and its design quality with unconventional vertical glass walls rising 50 feet high. The entire building has 15,000 square feet of glass and all horizontal surfaces are constructed of metal. The Jewel Box is surrounded by rose gardens and lily ponds. I have been there numerous times for it's an art deco floral conservatory.

For Tauriana, the choice of the Jewel Box was because it represents something special. Her personal and heartwarming reason was:

"Inside the Jewel Box, I feel the love with no boundary. It is a different feeling: no boundaries as the glass just lets everything show through. This helps you see that there is no limit to the love we can build together, sharing love with all the people who surround us, all our family and friends. Love has no boundaries..."

The Music for the Wedding

The moment we entered this transparent palace of love for the wedding, we noticed the distinctive difference from other weddings we have attended. A musician was playing a saxophone instead of the traditional piano or organ. Nor was there a choir or vocalist. We knew then Tauriana had a special request for the musician and the choice of her wedding music. Her explanation was,

"I know the saxophone musician through our sorority group. He played at our sorority functions. This time, as a special request for my wedding, I gave him the list of Stevie Wonder songs to play. My plan was to surprise Eli. Eli is a fan of Stevie Wonder and I knew that these songs would make him happy, comfortable, and relaxed."

After Eli was relaxed in the position where he stood while waiting for the ceremony to begin, the time for the entrance of the bride was near. While all the guests were waiting for Tauriana to appear and walk down the aisle with her father, a female singer sang the song, *"At Last."*

At Last

It was my very first experience to hear this popular and famous Etta James song at the wedding. *"**At Last**"* was a "first" for me. I knew it was something very special. Listening to every word in the lyrics that just said it all!

At last my love has come along
My lonely days are over
And life is like a song

At Last, the skies above are blue
My heart was wrapped up in clover
The night I looked at you

And here we are in heaven
For you are mine at last

151

Here Comes the Bride

After the vocalist finished the song, **"At Last"** all the guests turned their heads back to watch the entrance of the bride; yet, to all of our surprise, it was eleven friends of honor first, followed by the bride. Tauriana was walking down the aisle by herself. I was pleasantly surprised!! I knew then that this was the most unforgettable wedding in my life. Later, I learned about this extraordinary ceremony from Tauriana herself.

"Because my father is a preacher; he is already standing at the altar... My father has his own church in Michigan..." It was only then that I understood why she was walking down the aisle all by herself. Her father, the preacher did not walk with his daughter. After Tauriana shared with me how her decision was made, I began to see a very special woman.

"The reason I walked down the aisle by myself is because for me, this was my crossing over to the next stage of my life independently. Independence is very important to me because I have always been independent. But, symbolically, as I moved, I willingly let my self go so that I may begin to share myself in this journey with somebody else. So I have to walk by myself to meet the person with whom I am about to start the next step in my life. This was the time to take Eli's hand to walk down our journey together."

I couldn't help but wonder about the importance of being independent. I knew there was a special strong bonding with her father; yet, her father did not take part in the tradition of "giving the bride away." What was it about Tauriana's past that caused her to make an unconventional choice? When asked, Tauriana provided information about her childhood.

"My biological mother died of heart attack when I was only eight years old. My mom was only twenty-five years old at that time. I was adopted by my aunt and uncle. They never had a child so they were glad to raise me. I went to visit my father often, though. For my wedding, I felt like

I was too old to have lots of bridesmaids and groom's men, so all my friends were friends of honor." At that point, she stopped and looked at me. Then, she gave me a huge smile and said;

"I want you to be part of my life, and join in with all of my other friends of honor."

Preacher's Daughter

This was the first time I had witnessed the bride walking alone down the aisle after the bride's eleven friends of honor. The preacher, Tauriana's father, was smiling and watching his daughter walking down the aisle by herself independently. Tauriana explained to me about her special eleven bride's friends.

"At my wedding, my sorority sisters wore grayish color dresses. The color gray stands for stability and calm whereas Eli's favorite color is purple, like a peacock. So, with bright, purplish peacock color the men wore and calming grayish color the women wore, there was a good balance between Eli and me...

...all my sorority friends came to my wedding...You would never have known that some of the sorority members at my wedding didn't even know each other, because they meshed so well. You wouldn't have known that some had just met that day. Among them, nine of us who had known each other for a long time...

...There were about ninety sorority members. Half of my sorority members actually came from our college - Eastern Illinois University...

...When we finished college, we immediately became a part of Delta Sigma Theta Sorority, Inc. Our sorority members do community service until we die. We are all over the United States and other countries."

Delta Sigma Theta Sorority, Inc.

Tauriana has been working at the sorority where they offer community services around the East St. Louis area. They meet once a month and discuss up-coming events, budgets, and ideas to raise money for the things that they promised would be done.

"It was an amazing experience for all of us, and now we are friends. Next month, we will have our national convention in Washington D. C; it will be our 100th anniversary. So far, there are 36,000 members who have already registered."

Tauriana had lived in Chicago before coming to East St. Louis area in 2001.

"It was tough growing up in East St. Louis, a pretty rough area and people. They don't know how to get out of that situation. No means to get out..." Tauriana was in deep thought; then, she explained her thoughts and feelings on these issues.

"...We have the issue with The Haves and The Haves Not - some people have, some don't. You have to make the difference. We can't do it for them. All we can do as a sorority is to show them how to do for themselves...

I was in deep thought about how we grew up in Taiwan. My girlfriends from my three years at Taipei First Girls High School and four years in Sociology at Taiwan University have maintained an extremely strong bond ever since graduation. Many of us stay in close contact even today. What bonded us then was one single reason - we studied together literally every single day during those years in order to get into higher education. Yes, we all achieved that main goal in life. I now wish I could have done more. Learning about Tauriana's sorority members and what they have been doing since their graduation has given me incredible appreciation and admiration for what American culture has instilled in younger generations.

...At the Washington D. C; convention this year, we will elect a new President, and set the new challenges. We have partnered with the NAACP, and National Counsel for Negro Women." Tauriana flashed a big and proud smile.

Back to the Wedding: "You Are So Beautiful To Me"

Toward the end of the wedding ceremony, Eli and Tauriana turned around and faced the guests; then, they began walking away from the altar together. All of a sudden, her father, the preacher, sang from the altar.

You Are So Beautiful To Me
Can't you see... You're everything I hope for...
You're everything I need...

You Are So Beautiful To Me

Tradition: Jumping The Broom

The song was beautiful to all of us. Then, something else surprised me. Tauriana recounted,

"...My sorority friends held three ropes with three different colors: the gold one symbolized God; the white stood for purity and the purple represented strength. Then, Eli held one end and I held the other end, both of us braided three ropes together... Then, at the end of ceremony before leaving, we did the traditional Jumping the Broom. I made the broom...it is a tradition.."

"What tradition?" I asked.

"It is an African tradition that is symbolic of binding a couple in marriage and also can be used as a symbol of fertility and prosperity for the couple."

It was another tradition I had never heard of. I was very fascinated by this tradition and asked a history teacher friend of mine, who was very knowledgeable about this tradition.

*"It is an African custom for marriage. In Alex Haley's book, **Roots**, the jumping of the broom at the end of the wedding ceremony is explained. I think it originated in the mid-19th century as a practice among the slaves in the United States. Back in slavery days, they would jump the broom to symbolize the marriage. Most marriages between enslaved blacks were not legally recognized. As in law, marriage was held to be a civil contract, and civil contracts required the consent of free persons. The ceremony jumping of the broom served as an open declaration of settling down in a marriage relationship amongst African Americans...*

...I think in the South the custom used to determine who would run the household: whoever jumped highest over the broom was the decision maker of the household or whoever landed on the ground first after jumping the broom was predicted to be the decision maker in the marriage..." Then, he looked at me with mischievous smile and asked,

"Which one of your friends jumped highest or landed first, husband or wife?"

I smiled and told him that I remembered vividly that Tauriana had not indicated that the first to land on the ground would be the "bossy" one. Rather, she explained her view on jumping the broom. She said,

"To me, jumping the broom signified our union and how we were entering into a new life ...starting a new family by symbolically 'sweeping away' both of our former single lives, former problems and concerns. Therefore, Eli and I jointly entered a new adventure as wife and husband by jumping over the broom."

After the jumping the broom ceremony was over, every guest was asked to stand in front of the Jewel Box for a photograph. Tauriana said,

"The photograph was a symbol that everybody took part of this union that just happened. We chose the people who meant something to us in our life to walk this path together. That is important to us! "

Wedding Reception

There were twelve tables with eight guests at each table. Every one would get a pack of candy and looked for his/her table; each table was labeled with a different theme. I was anxious to discover which theme was chosen for Steve and me. Our names were under the theme of **Happy**. It was very interesting but I wondered how it came about.

"The themes all represent how you came into our lives. You and Steve remind me of happiness between you two. Other themes were: Magical, Eternity, Forgiveness, Love, Fate, Unity, Joy, Desire, Soul Mate, Loyalty, Trust and Commitment."

Also, the guests were asked to sign their names on a huge picture of Eli and Tauriana, not the traditional wedding book. Tauriana gave me her reason:

"Symbolically, the signing of the wedding picture joined everyone together for this union. I wanted to do things that are inclusive. Usually, when we go to a wedding, we just sign our names in the wedding book. So, I decided that I wanted every one to come together. Now, that huge picture of Eli and me has more meaning to us each time we see it. Looking at the picture brings back memories of the wedding but also reinforces the idea of the friends of honor that supported us on that special day.

The Wedding Dance

Their first wedding dance was the bride and the groom. It was followed by the family dance that, traditionally, would be the bride and her father. But Tauriana's choice was to include the instant family that was the result of this wedding. The kids from both sides danced together in a circle. The song for the family dance was called, "*Family Affair.*" Then, another pleasant surprise came when the third dance began. Tauriana had yet another explanation.

"*The third dance included all ladies here in St. Louis and those from Chicago. The name of the dancing song is Beyonce's song, "Love On Top.... the song is about being in love. I want to use this song to help Eli to understand how he makes me feel. So, I asked one of my sorority sisters to help me to choreographed.... The song "**Love on Top**" is about being in love. I wanted to use this song to help Eli to understand how he makes me feel....*

You're the one I love
You're the one I need
You're the only one I see

You're the one that gives your all
You're the one I can always call

When I need you make everything stop
Finally you put my love on top

.... Therefore, I asked my one of my sorority friends to help me choreograph and stage a dance to go with this song to show Eli how I felt about him... The group of eight sorority members practiced dancing steps for a couple of months before the wedding. I kept it secret by telling Eli that I exercised at gym, but, actually I was practicing with the sorority girls in preparation for the wedding. Every week, we came together and even learned to dance with our heels on. It was a production that bonded us together even more. Only friends of honor would give this much time."

Eli and Tauraiana created a great start with special symbols and meaningful moments. They kept the traditions, as demonstrated in the wedding ceremony, and show that diversity is alive and well in America.

Tauriana's friendship with her sorority members reminds me of Chinese old sayings:

* *Remember, no man is a failure who has friends.*
* *If you want to know someone's character, look at the friends he keeps.*
* *Good friends are like stars, you don't always see them, but you know they're always there.*

Pearls of Wisdom

Jayne Baulos

*"Be yourself – a totally true self – because you
can't keep up with the pretense.
Just be yourself when you are **with** others or **without.**"*

I will never forget these words spoken with true conviction by my dear friend Jayne (pronounced Janey). Our friendship began more than 25 years ago as a shared love of cooking and fine food and grew into a wonderful camaraderie. It all started when Jayne Baulos attended the second cooking class I taught at the Kitchen Conservatory in Clayton during mid 1990s. From the questions she asked and the comments she made during that class, I could tell her curiosity went far beyond than the ten ingredients Lo Mein. In fact, before the evening was done, we had already decided to meet for our first lunch to share stories and recipes.

Throughout the years, Jayne and I often met for lunch as an excuse for trying different interesting restaurants. In all those years, Jayne never ceased to amaze and inspire me with how she viewed life. At each get-together, she gave me pearls of wisdom that were sweeter than rice pudding.

Jayne is an inspiration to women everywhere. "Enrichment" and "nourishment" are two concepts Jayne strongly believed in and supported, especially for women who wished to further their education. She also had a passion for children in need of health care.

Even though she suffered from a painful health condition which limited her movement, she did not allow her disability to limit her involvement in various charities focused on addressing these important issues.

She was a remarkable woman who put into practice her personal beliefs. She raised two highly intelligent daughters who achieved more. One has a doctorate and teaches at the University of Las Vegas, and the other has a senior position in a firm in Washington D.C. They, in turn, are instilling those positive attributes on their talented, intelligent, musical and athletic children.

When I asked her what influenced her parenting and her involvement in community humanitarianism, she replied,

"The impetus stemmed from my great grandparents who came to St. Louis from Illinois in the late 1880s. They were builders and owned a big construction company. While they were building hospitals, schools, and other things, they were also instilling their strength of character and commitment to philanthropy in me."

Besides remaining actively involved with raising money for women, education, and disabled children who need prostheses, Jayne was also an active member of secret book club – a very unusual women's club. A few years ago, Jayne asked me to be the speaker at the club. I was shocked and asked "*Why me?*" She replied,

"Because of your cookbook, Fairy Tale Soup!"

"But, it is a cookbook, not literature." I said.

"In your book,: Jayne explained, *"Each recipe gives one page of background about the dish with either a personal story about yourself or cultural tidbits about being Chinese. That's what my book club members are interested in. We want to hear from you."*

After my presentation, I was so touched by these intelligent women, their culturally motivated and intriguing questions about my Chinese history, as well as their extensive knowledge of history and culture. Wanting to know more about them, I asked Jayne how she chose to become a member of this book club.

"I didn't choose them; they asked me after one of their members passed away."

"Only then?"

"Yes, there may be only 30 members at a time. This exclusive book club was established in the late 1880s. They invite new members only when one of their 30 passes away."

My admiration for Jayne did not stop there. She also had an amazing talent for making miniature dollhouses. She developed this passion when she was only 7 or 8 years old. Years later, when she was in her 50's, she was in a toy store buying a wedding gift, and a dollhouse caught her interest. She said to herself, *"I can do that, and maybe even better!"* Over the years she meticulously recreated miniature houses and "tableaux," capturing memories of years gone by. In 2011, she donated a 16-room dollhouse and more than 20 individual room boxes to the Miniature Museum of Greater St. Louis in South St. Louis City. One series of dollhouses consists of 12 different shops from 1904-1906: a hardware store, a bakery, a tearoom, an Italian grocery store, a greenhouse, a florist shop, and many others. All are shining gems to tickle the fancy.

Because of her experience and wisdom, Jayne was the one I sought out when I had questions about life. At lunch one day, I asked:

"One more question. If we didn't know each other, and I approached you as a total stranger for words of wisdom, what would you advise me?"

Without hesitation, her response was,

"Be yourself – a totally true self – because you can't keep up with the pretense. Just be yourself when you are with others or without."

As I walked her to her car, Jayne paused a moment to rest. Then, she turned around, looking at me for a few seconds, and said,

"Always look at the world on the bright side; there is enough bad out there without inviting more." Trying to catch her breath, she smiled and continued,

*"So, always see the good side of **each** situation."*

After years of struggling with poor health, in 2011, Jayne fell seriously ill with esophageal cancer. Her fight with the disease was long and taxing, but she never gave up her hope or her good humor. During the last two weeks of her life, I visited her almost daily. The last day I saw her, she said to me,

"I'm hungry."

"What do you want me to bring for you to eat tomorrow?" I asked,

She thought and thought, but before she could answer, I said,

"I know! Shrimp Toast! Your favorite!" Her eyes lit up and she smiled, content with the memory of so many shared meals.

Watching her slowly lose her brave battle against cancer, I could not help but be grateful that Jane had for so many years willingly and wholeheartedly shared her joy, her passion, and her words wisdom with me – like a priceless string of perfect, glistening pearls.

As Chinese old sayings:
*   **Pearls don't lie on the seashore. If you want one, you must dive for it.**
*   **Listen to wise advice, better than reading books for ten years.**

The Making of A Principal

Craig Fenner

When you pass through the doors of Parkway South Middle School, you are not just entering an academic institution. The warmth and openness of the building is more like that of a village - a village of caring, skilled educators who create an atmosphere of enlightenment and learning.

Welcome to the community we call Parkway South Middle School, where every student knows the principal. No, not for disciplinary reasons. Instead, Craig Fenner makes himself a visible presence, morning, noon, and night.

From the moment the school buses arrive, he watches all the kids get on and off the buses; he walks in the hallway and asks the kids to stop running or to keep their hands to themselves between classes; and he supervises students during each lunch hour by talking with the kids and walking around inside the cafeteria.

I know he has a soft spot for the children, but he also has a soft spot for Chinese food. Since Chinese cuisine is one of his favorite foods, I always bring a homemade lunch to share with him when I work as a substitute teacher after I retired. He smiles and eats the food during lunch as he watches kids in the cafeteria. He grins and nods while eating, and I know the fried rice or the cashew chicken are pleasurable to his palate.

After visiting different schools in St. Louis' West County, I've decided that each school's image shines through the bulletin boards displays. They reflect the school's culture and the character of its leadership.

In Mr. Fenner's middle school, the wall tells stories that are inspiring and motivating. It reflects the values cherished by Mr. Fenner on each bulletin board, the posters, note cards, and the art work. They are all created by the students under teacher's supervision. But, it is Mr. Fenner, the principal who discreetly leads and guides them by example.

Cafeteria: This is a multi-functional place where students eat lunch, parents and teachers hold meetings, and the orchestra, band, and choir perform. Next to the cashier, a large sign says *"Build a Healthy Lunch, Meat or Meat Alternative, Grains, Milk, and Fruits and Vegetables."* This encourages students -- consciously or subconsciously -- to make healthy choices when it's time to order lunch.

On the cafeteria wall, different messages are displayed for each season. On one visit, I saw several items that contributed to the "school/village" feeling. Each of the huge posters displayed was a collage of students' pictures. All pictures were taken by the students who were doing some kind of school activity, such as drawing, building, writing, or playing. In the center of each five collage was a single large word representing its theme : *Family, Knowledge, Learning, Friendship* and *Success.*

Above the collages is a TV displaying after-school activities, continuously running like TV commercials.

- o *Chess Club, Monday, Wednesday and Thursday in Room 1502, Mr. Kulick's room*
- o *Spirit Day*
- o *Shoeman Water Project Kick Off - Wear crazy socks and mismatched shoes and bring shoes to donate all month long*
- o *Japanese Club Every Monday - Students will learn beginning spoken and written Japanese. They will also explore various cultural aspects of Japan*

Counselor's Office: Outside the counselor and school policeman's office is a glass bulletin board. Under the words "Heart Quotes," there are heart-shaped cutouts, and each one features a counselor and student's favorite quote:

Marc Chagall - If I create from the heart, nearly everything works; if from the head, almost nothing.

Benjamin Franklin - The heart of a fool is in his mouth, but the mouth of a wise man is in his heart.

Antonio Porchia - In a full heart, there is room for everything, and in an empty heart, there is room for nothing.

Gym: Announcements line the walls.

Everyone is welcome. Already Know How to Play? Great! Join Us! New to Volleyball? That's great, too! Join us - It'll be fun!

POMS CLUB starts today!!! All grade levels and experience welcome. No need to sign up, just come to the mini gym after school.

Do you have a water bottle? Don't get caught without your water bottle.

7th Grade Hall: Posters made with colorful sheets of construction paper, hand made by 7th grade students, decorate both sides of the hallway:

Always try to Reach Your Goal No Matter What Anyone Says.

One piece of advice I have for 7th graders is Have fun and Enjoy Your Teacher!

When given the choice between being right and being kind, choose kind.

American History Class: In the hallway, next to the 8th grade history classroom wall, students made posters featuring their favorite quotes and pictures of American presidents. These are all facts, but not all facts have to be boring. The headline of one poster stated:

"Presidents are people too."

It is time for us to realize that we're too great a nation to limit ourselves to small dreams! - Ronald Reagan, 1911-2004

10 Fun Facts about George Washington:
o   *First President of the United States*
o   *First president to appear on a postage stamp*
o   *Fox hunting was George Washington's favorite sport*
o   *No one can buy a dollar bill without looking at George Washington*

Fun facts about America's 39th President Jimmy Carter:
o   *He won the 2002 Nobel Peace prize for advancing peace and human rights*
o   *He lost 30 pounds while in office*
o   *He ordered all the white house thermostats to be turned down to save energy*
o   *He was the first president to have been born in the hospital*

And, I even learned a few things about Bill Clinton:
o   *Clinton was voted president of his sophomore class*
o   *He wanted to be president since he was 5*
o   *He was the youngest governor of Arkansas*
o   *In 2nd grade, Clinton raised his hand in class so much that his teacher gave him a D in participation*

Science Class: When I saw the sign on the 8th grade science class door, it made me want to go in: *You are about to enter a Science Learning Zone.* In another science class, the signs were more "personal." On this classroom door, many 6"x6" cards are posted with only one or two words. By the time you finish reading all of them, you know the teacher and students are welcome.

Together, the cards read:

When you enter, this classroom, you are a scientist, you are explorers, you are loved, you are respected, you are the reason we are here!

Library News: The sign by the library door has only two words: *I read.*

There is one poster that says:

If you read 18 books or more nominated Mark Twain/Truman books, pass the quizzes with 80% or higher, and turn in a final reflective essay question, your name will be entered in a drawing for book bags and E-Reader.

There are other criteria and rewards if you read 12 - 15 books. The message is simple and clear: Reading is encouraged and rewarded.

Student Council: When I first saw a sign that read "*Wild About Stuco,*" it caught my attention because I didn't know what "Stuco" meant, later I learned it is short for "student council".

There are other smaller signs that read:
The Sponsors
General Board Members
6th Grade Executive Board
7th Grade Executive Board
8th Grade Executive Board

Mr. Fenner explained the meaning of Stuco to him, saying "*No parents, it's all students.*"

I wanted to know what the student council members did. He said;

"*Students in each grade select their own board executive. Those members of the Student Council then present and pursue ideas such as donations to charity.*"

Art & Music: Papier mache, pillow-sized "art snacks," like Hershey's, Skittles, Lay's Potato Chips, M&Ms, and Fritos, line the main hallway to the art and music rooms. These are all made by the students. Close to the music room, there are more papier mache sculptures – guitars, cellos, violins, and more.

Custodian office: Outside the custodian office door, several hand-written colorful posters made by students are featured.

o   *Happy Custodian Appreciation Day! Thanks for always lending a hand!*
o   *Thanks so much for keeping our school clean! We're so thankful for you!*
o   *You keep our school beautiful and you work so hard.*
o   *Belinda Jackson, You are Amazing!*

The last one is my favorite!

Principal's Office: There are only two posters in Craig Fenner's office:

*   *We must learn to live together as brothers or perish together as fools. - Rev. Martin Luther King, Jr.*
*   *Perseverance*

Getting to Know Craig Fenner

One day after school, I decided to get to know the leader of this middle school. Mr. Fenner agreed to be interviewed. He is a straightforward, no-nonsense kind of principal. And he is a busy man. I could sense that he always has a number of thoughts and ideas running through his head. I knew I could only have a small amount of his time.

"Did you know you would become a principal when you were growing up?"

"No, I had no idea. Actually I graduated from high school when I was 15 years old. I always attended Catholic schools from one to another wherever we moved. At age of 16, I entered the University of Missouri... Academics were no problem during middle school and high school... the work was manageable, but I did not develop those all-important study skills or habits at all. In high school, I could read, listen and retain

information...but once I started college I realized that I needed to do even more."

"What happened?"

"To be honest with you, I struggled for a couple of years in college because I did not know how to study...at that time, having fun was more important than study. So during my third year, my college advisor sat me down and said to me, 'This school might be too big for you. I am not sure you can do the work. You might consider going to another smaller college....

... So, I set out to prove that they were wrong about me! I turned myself around. I studied and studied...and graduated on time in 1982."

"What was your first job after college?"

"I was fortunate enough to get a job as business education teacher working at two Parkway junior high schools and a traveling teacher as a football coach at Parkway West High School."

"What did you teach in your junior high business education?"

"Back then, during the 80s, a business teacher was what we called a Technology Exploration teacher. It was old, old typewriter skills...key boarding. We made sure students could type fast, and the main goals were speed and accuracy for business letters, applications, documents and more. Well, after five years of that, I decided to do an administrative type of job... fortunately enough, there was an opening for an administrative internship. My main responsibility as an administrative intern was to supervise kids on buses and handle bus discipline. I was also responsible for conflict mediation. All of that gave me my start as an administrator..."

"How did you go from business teacher and coach to becoming an administrator?"

"I worked one year and one month as an administrative intern. To be honest with you, I had so much fun coaching the football team, I told my

boss that I wanted to step back and teach and coach full time. But, at that time, there was a reduction in force with the district; they had to lay-off teachers. Since I was the youngest teacher I was told that I could not have the position. My coordinator at the time called me on Friday evening and said, 'Craig, it seems to me that you won't have the job next year.'...

... But, fortunately, the following Monday, I got another phone call and was told that I got an offer to be a full-time administrative intern if that's what I wanted. So I had no choice in this situation."

"Why not?"

"Because prior to this, I said to myself, 'There is no way I want to be a principal.' But I think the 'MAN' upstairs guided me there to have the perfect job. I worked as an administrative intern at a middle school for five years and at Fern Ridge High School until there was an opening position for an assistant principal. I took it and was in that position for seven years."

"So, that was an assistant principal position... then, how did you get to be principal?"

"Well, when I was an assistant principal, I swore I would never be a principal."

"Why not?"

"It's just perception. It would not fit me, the responsibility factor..."

What factor? I wondered.

"One time, what the assistant superintendent told me stuck with me. He said that in order to be an efficient principal, I needed to be fluent in math, social studies, science...I thought there is no way I could be efficient in all subject matters. But, the more I learned about the job as principal, the more I learned that I might have weaknesses in some of those academic areas, but I could manage my weaknesses because with my strengths."

"Could you share your strengths with me?" I smiled and told him, "*You don't need to be humble here.*"

"I can have people to support me, I can manage my weakness. I think one of my strengths is to hire good teachers. During the interview process, I follow my gut instinct. My gut tells me this person should be in this building or not in this building."

I was excited about what he said because of a particular teacher he had hired last year.

"Oh yes, you are right! Mrs. Schumacher is one of the best teachers that I have ever known. When I saw her for the first time in your building, I knew you were a good principal."

Diana and I worked together at a program where she was excellent in every way.

"Besides hiring the best teachers, what other qualities should a principal possess?"

"I think I am a good listener. Sometimes kids are so hurt, the principal does not listen. Some principals think they have to do everything. We can't do everything. I think teachers are the ones who should run the school. I believe in giving the teachers the opportunity to have the leadership. I don't consider myself the smartest one, but I have found the best teachers. **Principals are the ones who always reflect, always think about what they can do to make it better for the kids.**"

"Do you think your parents had a direct impact or influence on your career?"

"My father was a factory worker; when he was in his mid 20's, he had an accident in a car that was hit by a train. His legs went severely injured, one of his leg was amputated before he died...he died of cancer in his late 30s. One of my fond memories before he died, he sat in his chair, he

talked to his five children, one by one. When it was my turn, I remembered he just gave me a big hug, whispering in my ear and said, 'I love you!'"

At that moment, I felt very connected with Craig Fenner. What he just shared with me reminded me of my own personal experience.

"Wow! Mr. Fenner, I can't believe this! I had a very similar situation. When my father died, I was 13 years old and not doing well in school, almost failing. Five days before my father passed away, he talked to his five children ranging from 17 to 9, one by one. When it was my turn, he was holding my hand by his hospital bed, then, he whispered in my ear and said to me: Obey your mom. Study in America someday."

I told Mr. Fenner that I did "obey" my mother and fulfilled my father's wish to come to America. What a small world! I am a Chinese woman who came to America for higher education. And here I was talking with an African-American middle school principal whom I greatly admired.

Out of curiosity and respect, I asked,

"What was your father's message to you?"

*"One word: '**Perseverance!**' Stay in school, do not quit, do something positive for society. Actually, 'perseverance' is my mantra."*

I looked around his office and saw his **Perseverance** poster again, which suddenly had special meaning. It reminds me this famous Chinese proverb in perseverance:
* ***Perseverance can reduce an iron to a sewing needle.***

"What will be your legacy to your three adult children?"

*"**Enjoy life. Live your life to the fullest.** I may have gone overboard on my career, spending too much time on my career, not enough with my family, so I want them to enjoy life. **Money does not equal success. I want them to be successful by contributing to society.**"*

For Craig Fenner, his father's words and presence are felt in all he does. As principal, he pays it forward to all teachers and students. The walls of "his" school encourage both teachers and students alike to become all that they can be, and to never give up trying.

On that day, as I was leaving Parkway Middle School, Mr. Fenner's words about his father and his role as principal, one Chinese old saying came to me:

* *To forget one's ancestor's wisdom of words is to be a book without a source, a tree without root.*

The More I Read, I More I Know....!!!!!

Donna Pelikan

In 2010, I joined my four siblings for a family reunion in Taiwan, where we were raised. We toured the area and saw some buildings that were built or renovated after we left. After taking photographs of various monuments, we decided that we would each visit our old high school.

As I walked into my school, First Girls High School at Taipei, Taiwan. I was greeted with a nod by the security guard. He did not question my presence there, apparently, seniors are still trusted and respected in Taiwan.

As soon as I was inside the school building, I walked directly to my freshmen classroom on the second floor. Nothing had changed. It was a step back in time. Everything was exactly the same as when I was a student: the same chalkboard, the same desks and chairs arranged in straight rows. I felt like I was in a time machine. A couple of girls were in the classroom studying. They were dressed in the same uniform I used to wear – a green shirt with a black pleated skirt.

It was a Saturday morning.

I recalled sitting in that same classroom with my five best friends during the weekends, we studied together nearly 40 years before. On that day, there was one girl sitting in the same place that I used to sit:

fifth chair from the front in the second row by the window. I smiled and quickly introduced myself to her:

"Do you know I sat in the same chair in the sixties? What are you studying?"

"Oh, oh...wow! " She was stunned and replied humbly, *"Chinese Literature."* With the utmost respect, she politely handed me her Chinese Literature textbook.

Thumbing through this thin textbook, I was taken aback. It was just one half-inch thick with 15 short lessons. Looking at the chapter titles, I thought I was in an old, old country. Each lesson was only three-and-a-half pages long; the contents were about politics, thousand-year old literature, some Confucian philosophy, poetry, and Taoism. No romance, no adventure, no humor, no modern authors.

It was the same information I had learned. It was the same information that the entire country learned. It was 2010, but it could have been 1990, or maybe even 1960.

***************   ***************   ***************

Mrs. Donna Pelikan has been my close friend ever since 2000, when we both taught at Alternative Discipline Center in St. Louis County. Her classroom was the last one in the building. As you walked down the hallway toward her room, you could hear her students chanting. As you approached, the sounds became louder and louder:

The more I read, the more I know. The more I know, the smarter I grow. The smarter I grow, the stronger my voice when speaking my mind and when making a choice!

If the students didn't chant loudly enough, they were asked to repeat it. I found it interesting that they were smiling while they chanted, and they looked confident.

After the trip to Taiwan, I returned to St. Louis with a burning desire to learn more about Donna whose strong belief in education reminded me of Chinese cultural value. She was born in America and has lived in St. Louis her entire life. What drove her to become a reading specialist? What prompted her to teach in her particular style, with mantras and creativity?

Donna explained her philosophy about teaching anyone to read.

"I believe that no matter what is taught at any level in school, everything revolves around reading: learning how to read, reading to learn, reading in all of the content areas." She stopped for a moment, then added,

"Reading is essential for learning. Period! When I realized there were so many kids with so many issues that affected reading, I decided it was time for me to specialize and work all day, every day, teaching kids how to read." She continued:

"The biggest deal is getting kids excited about reading." That's her strategy. But, how does she motivate students, I wondered.

When we first met, it was in an alternative school program. These students have a variety of emotional issues, family problems, and learning challenges that made reading difficult for them. It was Donna's job to help them read so they could finish high school. But she did much more than that. She gave them the confidence to succeed and to see that life consists of many choices over which they have control.

"Chanting is to remind them that the more they read, the smarter they get and the smarter they become, the more prepared they are to make the right choices, especially in their troublesome teenage years." Donna paused, then added:

"Chanting reinforces the concept through auditory input."

179

Character Reading

Other than chanting, Donna got her students excited about reading by encouraging them to analyze characters in short stories and books. She explained:

*"Guiding students through character analysis helps reveal their thoughts about life as they compare actions and possible motives. Students live vicariously through the characters in the books and provide insight into their thoughts. **Discussing the characters in the books and stories provide the opportunity to listen and learn from others in a safe, non-judgmental environment."***

She also believes that a student's reading level is not necessarily indication of their intellectual ability. She has known physicians and engineers who can comprehend scientific material flawlessly, yet cannot detect sarcasm, symbolism, or abstract meaning in a novel.

Donna motivated students using an accelerated reading program that motivated students to increase their reading levels. First, they chose books at their own level, but then moved on quickly to more difficult material as they learned to answer more complex questions. By choosing their own reading material, students controlled their own choices, which also helped them to stay out of trouble.

One collection, in particular, especially excited the students' interest, J.K. Rowling's Harry Potter. It was the book she used to introduce the students to the class. They learned that the author wrote the books as an unemployed single mother, sometimes even using toilet paper to record great ideas. To help kids conceptualize the books, Donna also let them listen to the audio version. The audio book narrator was able to bring the book to life by changing his voice for each character. That captivated the students and helped them imagine the story. She shared her teaching strategy reason with me and said,

"Each student chose their own books at their own level. The lessons became interesting because they didn't just 'read,' they studied characters."

Her motivational teaching style profoundly affected one eighteen-year-old senior. His mother was a physician who informed Mrs. Pelikan that he had been diagnosed with a learning disability in reading.

On the first day that students were allowed to choose their own books, this student told her,

"I don't read books. I always listen to them on tape."

Donna directed the student to choose a book anyway based on the introduction. The student chose Walter Dean Myer's book, *Monster,* for the class. The novel is about a sixteen-year-old boy accused of murder. Donna explained to the student:

"I don't have money for books on tape. You'll have to wait for me to tape each chapter. Then, you can listen to it." (This was before audio books were widely available.)

She said she paused for a moment at that time and then told the student:

"Or, you can read out loud by yourself until I can get the recordings prepared."

The student thought for a while. Then, he said:

"Ok! Mrs. Pelikan, I'll give it a try! "

After two days, the student finally decided to read the book by himself. Every day during lunch, he came to Mrs. Pelikan's classroom to read. All reading time for students was done either in class or after lunch during free time. This young man chose to read in Mrs. Pelikan's room at lunch. He sat on the floor, resting his back against the wall for twenty to thirty minuets each day. At the end of three weeks, he slapped the book and closed it loudly. He then announced:

"This is the first book I have read word for word, all by myself since sixth grade."

The next semester, he received a very high score in reading on the ACT that allowed him to attend the college of his choice.

Mrs. Pelikan told her students that they had the necessary intelligence, but lacked practice in reading. She used sports, like football, to provide an analogy the students could understand.

*"**No matter how good the coach is or how many videos a player watches, he will not improve unless he practices**,"* she said. By talking about how practice benefits athletes, Donna was able to motivate her students. She said:

"Coaches have their teams practice core activities. Through practice, the players are better prepared for any formation or situation. It's the same in reading. The more you do it, the better you become."

Mrs. Pelikan believes that teachers must do more than just coach. Teachers must believe in their students.

Believing In Them!

Donna recalled one transfer student. When she first met "Mary," she thought that the girl looked much older than her years. *"Mary"* was 5' 7" and weighed nearly 200 pounds. She had a wonderful smile and a pleasant demeanor. One day, *"Mary"* came to school with two black eyes. She claimed she had fallen out of bed. Donna knew it was more than that. She gave her a lot of sympathy, encouraging *"Mary"* to talk with the school counselor. Meanwhile, this student helped Mrs. Pelikan with chores around the classroom, and chose to stay inside during recess whenever possible to read. Apparently, she felt safe and comfortable in Mrs. Pelikan's room. That Christmas, "Mary" brought some earrings and gave them to Mrs. Pelikan and she still has the earrings till today.

Another transfer student had a very difficult time with oral and written communication. Journal writing was one of the ways Mrs. Pelikan taught the students how to communicate in a non-threatening way. Journal entries also helped Mrs. Pelikan learn about her students because personal reflections were part of the assignment. The following journal exchange shows how the process worked.

One day, *"Jane"* wrote in her journal:
"My uncle died."
"How did he die?" Mrs. Pelikan wrote in the journal.
"He died," Jane wrote again.
"How did your uncle die?" Mrs. Pelikan asked.
"He died," Jane wrote again.
"Where were you?" Mrs. Pelikan asked.
"He died," Jane repeated.
"Did you see him die?" Mrs. Pelikan asked.
"He got shot," Jane wrote.

After that brief conservation, *"Jane"* started writing about the incident. From then on, she opened up to Mrs. Pelikan. They carried on longer and longer conversations, and she read more and more.

Singing Along with Reading

Mrs. Pelikan is very flexible in her teaching. She saw students respond to different approaches as they grew. Throughout her years of teaching, from kindergarten through college, she has utilized fun and engaging approaches.

Younger children responded to reading guru Dr. Tim Rasinski's, **Sing Along!** In Rasinski's system, kids learn about sound-symbol relationships, phrasing and meaning without even realizing it as they sing along. Being a creative person, Mrs. Pelikan took it a step further by singing in French. Mrs. Pelikan explained,

"This helps me to understand if the kids could hear and imitate sounds they heard as opposed to using memory. Then, we would translate to English which was no big deal because the songs were usually familiar, like 'Silent Night."

"What about intermediate readers like second through sixth grade? " I asked.

"Those kids like computerized programs that involve fact-based tests about books they have read. The programs are very concrete. Students work at their own pace and move up levels based on their success. kids love, and are motivated by the idea of moving up on the color-coded levels."

The parents were so impressed with the progress of their children that they bought books for the program so that the students would have a wider variety of choices.

The Puppet Show

While teaching elementary school, Mrs. Pelikan staged puppet shows with her students. She built a puppet stage out of painted cardboard. The students created the puppets. The play was based on *The Whipping Boy*, an award-winning book by Sid Fleischmann that had difficult British language structure. Mrs. Pelikan recorded the show on video. Recording the performance was a key element because it allowed the students to see themselves and evaluate their performance.

"They got lots of practice because they read over and over without realizing it." she said.

Even though the story was written in an old English dialect with challenging vocabulary, the students were so focused on the performance that they never got tired of repeating a scene to make the video look good. As a result of so much repetition, the kids' vocabulary improved markedly. Mrs. Pelikan's methods were innovative, but grounded in research showing that repetition helped students to learn.

What was the plot of *The Whipping Boy?* I wondered.

"This award winning author combines comedy with deep compassion in this novel about a Prince and a Pauper. The two boys have nothing in common, but were taken hostage together after running away," Mrs. Pelikan said, *"Their escapades contain universal components about human nature that all kids understand."*

"Wow! This is the first time I ever heard about this story! But, in elementary school? Kids read this kind of material? Hostages? Running away? What is the moral of the story? " I asked. I couldn't help but wonder why this kind of story was being taught at the elementary school level in America.

"This tale combines high adventure with suspenseful and colorful characters." Mrs. Pelikan answered.

Her story brought back the memory of my first grade reading class at East Gate Elementary School in Taipei. Teacher Lin required us to read out loud by chanting together everyday.

The very first lesson that the fifty of us were asked to read together was:

Come! Come! Come! Come to School!

Even today, the sound of chanting still freshly remains in my memory vividly. At the age of six, we didn't know we were being "programmed" to value the importance of education by studying. We did what our teachers asked without explanation. But, I don't think we ever smiled while we were all reading out loud. There was no singing along. No puppet show either. Reading was a serious matter. Studying was even more serious than anything else in my first grader's mind and soul.

While I was deep in thought, Mrs. Pelikan got up and said that she wanted to show me something. It was a quilt that she had made with her 3rd grade students.

Quilt Together!

A six feet by five feet dark blue flowered quilt was made of twelve inch squares. In the center of the quilt, there are twenty eight six-inch white squares of fabric. Each one is a student's painting based on the book, *Charlotte's Web* by E.B. White. There were so many patches: the spider's web, the author's name, the characters, the little girl named Fern, the friendship between the pig and the barn spider. Donna brought her sewing machine to class. Mrs. Pelikan sewed the quilt together while her 3rd grade students were reading the story.

Looking at this big colorful quilt with its twenty eight patches, I was literally speechless. I have never met another reading teacher who would go so far as to bring her own sewing machine to school and make a quilt about the book her students were reading.

She pointed to one of the small squares of fabric, representing a student's drawing. On the left hand corner was written, "*I am going to be your friend*" and on the right side, it read, "*I'm Wilbur!*"

Later I learned that Mrs. Pelikan gave one class quilt to a little boy whose father suffered a fatal heart attack after bringing his children to school. By giving the class quilt, she demonstrated her belief in teaching: generosity, caring and compassion.

Mutual Understanding!

I look at my thin book from my high school in Taiwan. Thin though it is, its writings encompass the structure of Chinese culture.

Mrs. Pelikan is an American educator who encourages students to explore, find their own ways, create and look beyond.

Why are they so different? I wondered. I try to understand why they are so different.

America is such a young culture, and was built by immigrants who shared their own cultures and heritages.

One day, I decided to ask one of my high school friends about our Chinese culture and heritage. She provided an answer that I had never thought of, yet it made a lot of sense. She explained:

"From elementary school to high school, most Chinese Language or Literature teachers required us to memorize a short lesson after giving us the brief explanation about the content which fundamentally was about our traditional cultural values in recognition of the eight virtues - piety, fraternal duty, loyalty, faith, propriety, righteousness, frugality and shame. It doesn't matter whether it was written as poetry, thousand-year- old literature or philosophy or even historical events...

...We have five thousand years of history, culture and heritage. Teachers expected all students to learn all of that within twelve years from elementary to high school, then someday, with enough life experiences, we would have some 'ah- ha moments' in which these virtues would show us how to live. Therefore, while still young, we memorized the virtues so that we could use them in our lives, whenever those 'ha- ha moments' would happen."

It was my first "ah-ha moment." I realized I might officially be considered as a slow learner by our Chinese standards. But, by American standards, it is never too late to learn.

As a reading specialist, Mrs. Pelikan always searches for new methods to address each student's needs. She believes that all of us have different talents, but basic human values as well. We acknowledge that which unites us, while appreciating our different talents. On the bulletin board in her reading class, one poster read,

Celebrate the difference. Appreciate the similarity.

In Chinese culture, the youth are taught the edicts that have promoted and instilled the same culture and civilization down through the ages, over thousands of years.

In American culture, edicts are overlooked in favor of strategies that focus on individualism, scientific technology, humor, motivation, personal adventures, empathy and student-centered methodology.

As Chinese proverbs say:
* *A nation's treasure is in its scholars.*
* *A book holds a house of gold.*

Postscript:

Donna currently serves on the Reading Success Center board, a non-profit organization that serves underprivileged struggling readers in the St. Louis Region. She also works part time with Reading Plus, a software program that helps students increase reading comprehension, vocabulary, and silent reading fluency. Donna continues to train teachers and help students improve their skills while increasing their love for reading.

The Music Man

Mike Holdinghaus

***Hartford Coffee House**, one block south of Tower Grove Park*

The first time I heard the term "hootenanny" I really did not know what to think. After years of living in America, I was very confident in my English. So many words. So much work on my part. I had done a pretty good job learning American English. Now, it seemed there was a new vocabulary word. Was this a word inspired by owls? Where did it come from? Imagine my surprise when I learned that "hootenanny" was a musical party.

Soon, I found out that the power of hootenanny goes beyond words. It can help change thoughts, ideas, or even societies. Mike Holdinghaus brought me to my first hootenanny. And, for many years, he has helped open the door to music across St. Louis, especially at the Hartford Coffee House near Tower Grove Park.

Mike Holdinghaus, the Orchestrator

Mike reminisced as he talked about his favorite philosopher and his fiftieth birthday party:

*"Viktor Frankl is a philosopher I admire. Frankl said, '**We are the happiest when we find deep meaning in what we do**'"*

How did one of Victor Frankl's quotes inspire him to perform at the Hartford Coffee House? Why did Mike, the music man, decide to orchestrate the neighborhood hootenannies?

I wondered.

"When turning 50 years old, I decided to have a two-day birthday party, over a Friday and Saturday at my house. Because some friends worked on Saturday, I asked my musician friends to come to my house any time during those two days to sing. Also, I love to cook. For two days straight, my friends came to sing and eat my food. We would either sing alone or together...We sang songs written by Bob Dylan, who is my favorite singer and composer. We all had a blast!...

An Idea Reaches a Crescendo

... My friends and I had such fun just singing on my 50ᵗʰ birthday party, I thought, why couldn't we just keep singing and invite others to join us, at a public place perhaps? Why couldn't we enjoy singing the songs we love once a month at the Hartford Coffee House, which is just around the corner? And, not have to wait until my 60ᵗʰ birthday! We have been hanging out ever since, singing together for more than ten years."

"With some rules!" He added:

"No one gets paid. We avoid politics or religion, and there is no competition among the musicians. People from the neighborhood come to enjoy music performed by musicians who love performing every third Saturday night. And, I'm told, that night is one of the most profitable nights for the owner of the coffee house. So it's a win-win situation. This is exactly what W. Edwards Deming, the economic philosopher meant when he said:

When we cooperate and work together to make high quality products, everyone benefits."

What is Mike Holdinghaus' own philosophy behind the neighborhood orchestra? Mike reflected on his years as a teacher and the role music played in teaching students how to succeed, he said:

"I was a history teacher for twenty years at the elementary level and spending eleven years in middle schools. It was important to me to make the environment one in which the students would surprise themselves with how much they could succeed... I played music for each class. It was mostly recorded music but sometimes I played my guitar. I am not good at playing guitar, but my students tolerated it. The excitement my students felt when music was added to the class, it gave me confidence to go forward with the hootenannies. After all, the hootenannies use music to tell a story, much like history. The students' love and appreciation of music gave me the confidence to be where I am with the hootenannies."

Mike was very touched by the impact he had on his students. Using one example, he recalled:

"I was at a funeral when a young man walked up to me and excitedly told me that he remembered my playing guitar in the classroom thirty years ago. How powerful is that to a teacher?"

Being a Teacher

*"**I believe in students**. All those years as a teacher, **I de-emphasized grades and I emphasized learning, and not to learn for money. I believe that everyone has a voice.** Everyone should know what he can do and do the best he can. Every student can feel free by listening to music and can express their feelings through music. It helps many students have a deeper understanding of the subject. I wanted my students to feel respected, and it didn't matter whether they were rich, poor, white, black, straight or gay. **I believe that students have the right to develop to their greatest potential and be happy.** To me, **it is the fundamental understanding of human dignity. This is what I love about my country. It is what America is all about — true democracy!"***

191

When I asked him what music or which composer exemplified his teaching philosophy of what America stood for, his answer was:

"The president that best exemplified the concept of democracy was Harry Truman. He came to office relatively poor and left that way. His wife Bess and he took a road trip after he left office and stayed in inexpensive motels because he wouldn't cash in on his time in office. He was a good, modest man."

When President Truman was introduced in Mike's history class, Mike would play songs from Truman's era to explain the meaning of democracy and Truman's political beliefs. Mike continued:

"The songwriter who best expressed the idea of democracy was Woody Guthrie in his song, 'This Land is Your Land.' Pete Seeger is another songwriter who showed that a simple life of sharing uplifting music is a good way to live. He wrote, 'Where Have All the Flowers Gone?' which warns young people not to blindly follow government authority."

Playing Guitar to Teach History

Mike always brought his guitar to the classroom and began playing before class started as students were entering the classroom. When the kids walked in, they were excited about hearing the music. He explained to me about his teaching experiences and his beliefs:

"I taught in Missouri elementary schools in St. Louis, Cape Girardeau, Sullivan, Fulton, and St. Charles and at North Kirkwood Middle School. In each school, I played music to enhance the lessons. I thought it was important that students were exposed to good art and music, as well as to the curriculum...

*...John Holt is another philosopher who has had a strong impact on me. He said, '**Living is learning**' and when kids are living fully, energetically and happily, they are learning a lot, even if we don't always know what it is. At the Hartford Coffee House, I see people, young and old, just happy*

being there and enjoying playing and listening to music. I see myself as a conductor who uses community brainpower to organize people from all walks of life, encouraging them to express their passion in music. Some are very talented, some may not be as talented as others, but all are equally appreciated and encouraged. It is the same thing I did when I was a classroom teacher. The technique applies to public gatherings as to the classroom."

Mike is truly an admirable teacher who loves to bring out the best in each student by using his personable teaching method to illustrate American history. Personally, I find his methodology and educational philosophy to be unique and more phenomenal than anything I have seen in classrooms of other history teachers.

Mike continued to explain his rationale for using music as a teaching tool:

"Well, think about the kids for a moment! When students hear the music the moment they walk in, what do they expect?"

He made his point, but what kind of music did he choose to play in the classroom? Mike gave me the answers. I was very impressed and touched.

"It depends on what event or era I was about to teach. Ken Burns' documentary - The Story of American Music - offers a great deal of teachable material, from the Civil War to the 1929 crash, as well as Jazz, WWII era songs and so many others. For example, when learning about the Civil War, I used the song, 'Kingdom Coming.' It is an American Civil War song written and composed by Henry Work in 1862. Before the Emancipation Proclamation, this song was the celebration of promised freedom to slaves whose masters had been scared away by the Union military forces. When I showed the Ken Burns Civil War documentary, students could hear the song played as background music as a lively instrumental. Another example, when teaching the events before and after WWII, I played the Big Band Swing songs and lively 'Boogie Woogie Bugle Boy.' Kids got kick out of that fun song...

*...As a history teacher, **I believe America is an unfolding story about common people who come here to live and become powerful.** Our country, the United States of America, began with the notion that only the king or the president had the power. During early 40s, Norman Rockwell created four oil paintings: Freedom of Speech, Freedom of Worship, Freedom from Want and Freedom from Fear. They speak loudly about what we stand for."*

Those four paintings that Mike referred to reappeared in my memory. It was during my freshmen year in high school when the art teacher introduced art, she brought up pictures of Rockwell's famous paintings. We thought art was not included among the subjects for the College Entrance Examination in Taiwan, so we just shrugged it off. Now hearing from Mike, I began to connect the dots about the fundamental idea of freedom in American history, especially these four freedoms. Surprisingly, it stirred up my interest about American government for the very first time since I had prepared for the exam to become an American citizen. Some people, like me, who came from other countries sometimes take the true meaning of freedom for granted. At that moment, Mike gave me a very valuable private lesson about American history. He explained:

"Norman Rockwell's famous paintings actually were inspired by President Roosevelt's 1941 speech in which he listed the four freedoms – Freedom of Speech, Freedom of Religion, Freedom from Want, and Freedom from Fear. Aaron Copland wrote 'Fanfare for the Common Man' in 1942, partially in response to the US entry into WWII. Personally, I find that music very powerful! Rockwell was inspired by the famous speech by Vice President Henry Wallace, who proclaimed the beginning of the 'Century of the Common Man.' Our country stands for democracy."

Mike paused and contemplated in silence. Then, he shared his thoughts from his life experiences.

"I grew up in relative poverty compared to the people around us... I remember when there was no heat in the house, we stood around the

stove to get warm. Even so, I felt we had plenty and felt we were free. My mother was a cheerful woman who never spoke any ill words about anyone. She was hospitalized for lengthy periods while I was growing up. Because my mother was often not able to function, my father and his fireman friends hung around with us a lot, usually two to three times a week...

...That's the time I knew that when I became a teacher, I wanted my students to feel free from being judged by the others because of the clothes they wear, color of their skin, home situation, or sexual preference! We are all common people. That's why when you hear the trumpet played at the beginning of Aaron Copland's 'Fanfare for Common Man,' you will be touched by the sound of trumpet to salute the common people, not the King."

Mike picked up a pen and drew a triangle on a piece of paper. Tapping the point on the top of the triangle, he said:

"This is where the king or the president used to be in the political hierarchy -- with the common people at the bottom."

Drawing another triangle, but upside down this time, he said:

"But, in Jefferson's and Adam's and Madison's idea of a real democratic country, the triangle shape should be upside down, like this. The president should be at the bottom to serve his people; the common people are the top priority."

At that moment, I realized that I was given an unforgettable lesson by a wisest American history teacher.

A Very Wise American History Teacher

Both Mike and I were both school teachers. We agreed that each teacher's values and educational purpose is reflected in the pictures posted in the classroom. Mike's perspective on history was amazing.

He called one set of the posters in his classroom the *Wall of Heroes*. He used black and white photos of great American leaders such as Abraham Lincoln, Teddy Roosevelt, Martin Luther King, Jr. He posted them on windows so that sunlight would illuminate their faces. Other posters showed famous quotes. One in particular quoted Thomas Jefferson:' ***One cannot be both ignorant and free.***' Mike nodded and agreed by saying, "***In America, Freedom is cherished.***"

Being a Father

"As a father of two daughters, I wanted them to love music and to be all around musicians. Both took violin while growing up. The oldest, Clare-Noel, now works at Americorp. Her expertise is setting up environments during emergencies for men, women, and children displaced by the disaster. She still plays the fiddle for fun. My younger daughter graduated from Sydney, Australia with a double major, one in cognitive science and one in creative writing. She now is using those skills as a writer/designer and creates scenarios with problems which the gamers have to solve for a board game. Both daughters have learned from me that we owe it to the people around us to make our environment something to enjoy."

What can you learn at a hootenanny?

Each musician comes to the Hartford hootenannies for one purpose only: to share his or her talents and pure love for music with the people from the neighborhood. Everyone brings their own instruments. The variety of talent, as well as everyone's skill in expressing it, is fascinating. **That is what a hootenanny is all about: people entertaining and inspiring others**. Mike keeps that spirit alive by teaching, performing and sharing. Whether its Bob Dylan's 'Blowin' in the Wind,' Little Richard's "*Long Tall Sally*," or "*Ave Maria*," the hootenanny at the coffee house always brings something new to everyone.

After hearing his explanation about what motivated him to orchestrate the Hartford Hootenannies in the first place, it is clear that he is the main attraction, a true Music Man! His concept for bringing all musicians to the coffee house once a month is far wider than all the musical notes combined. He is not only talented for playing various instruments, but he also is a conductor, an organizer, and a great teacher.

The Music Man is Mike Holdinghaus

In the Chinese culture, he would be respected as a truly wise man. Mike found a new way to teach history by incorporating music. In doing this, he gave his students hope and peace. Mike does everything with his whole heart and shows in the reactions of his students and his audience.

Here are quotes from Confucius, a 2000-year old philosopher:
* *Reviewing what you have learned and learning anew, you are fit to be a teacher.*
* *Education breeds confidence. Confidence breeds hope. Hope breeds peace.*

What Does World Needs Now?

Sarah Yancey

My sister and I chat routinely over the phone. She lives near Paris - a seven -hour time difference - but we often talk in the afternoons. Some days, an event will change all that and we will talk immediately.

I called Ming Ming as soon as I heard about the tragic events in Paris. Terrorists had attacked a Kosher grocery, leaving several people dead. The French government and police were searching for three suspects. Television news was awash with coverage.

"Are you okay? What's going on there?"

I was also very concerned about my niece, Anna, and her French husband who actually live in the city. My sister lives in Viry-Chatillon, about a 40-minute Metro commute from Paris so Ming Ming was not close to the danger.

"We are fine...but there are many stores closed right now..." Ming Ming's voice began to fade away. Silence filled our conversation, then I heard her murmuring,

"...What are we going to do with the terrorists? ...How do you prevent that?"

Ming Ming sounded hopeless. After our phone talked, I thought about her question. Here we are, two sisters who have lived in different countries for more than 40 years. Now, both France and America are dealing with these horrific issues.

Civilization is being challenged. Intercultural/interracial education is needed. As I thought, instantly, a friend's name came to my mind -- Sarah Yancey.

Sarah and I taught for nearly two decades at the same public school - Parkway South High. Sarah was always involved in helping students broaden their knowledge through understanding of different cultures. Current events took me back to the day she approached me in the hallway near her classroom many years ago. She said to me,

"I need you to speak with a Chinese mother because she has many questions about Russia."

"Mandarin or Cantonese?" That is all I asked. It turned out, the student's mother and I spoke the same dialect.

Russia-Chinese Connection

Ever since I've known Sarah, she has supported American Field Service foreign exchange students. Years ago, U.S. Congress passed the Freedom Support Act to benefit foreign student exchanges. In 1995, our school sent eight American students to Russia for three weeks and welcomed ten students from Russia to our school.

The programs had a leader from each country. Both American and Russian leaders worked together to develop a common curriculum unit to be taught. The chosen students had to be high school level. One of our school's students was a young, ethnic Chinese named, Sonny. Sarah needed my translation skills for Sonny's mother. Sarah said to me;

"Sonny is very excited about the idea of going to Russia and wants to learn more about it. His mother isn't sure about letting her son go to Russia... Can you explain it to his mother?"

Speaking in Mandarin, I was able to build a rapport with Sonny's mother that allowed us to speak frankly, with great emotion. Her questions and concerns were understandable. As a Chinese mother myself, I understood that any mother would have the same basic fear in the same circumstance. Since Stalin's death in 1953, the political relationship between China and Russia had been rocky and intense. Sonny's mother anxiously expressed her concerns.

"You know, Russia does not like us. Will Russians threaten my son because he is Chinese?"

I explained to this stressed and frightened Chinese mother that American government policy operates to protect American citizens, especially foreign exchange students. She leaned forward, looked straight in my eyes, and whispered.

"How about Mrs. Yancey?"

"The most respectful and trustworthy teacher!" I responded instantly.

A genuinely warm smile of relief appeared on her face; she put both her hands together, bowed, and thanked me profusely.

On a recent afternoon, Sarah and I were sipping tea at my house, catching up on each other's lives after we retired. While reflecting upon the days we taught at South High, Sonny's name came up in our conversation. Sarah had just received great news from him. But first, she filled me in about that trip to Russia 20 years ago.

"Sonny was very smart, reliable, and dependable. Socially, he had limited experiences. He had never been to the theater, or the symphony, or had other typical experiences...

...After three weeks in Russia, the Russian students wanted to host a party for the American students and show off American music like Michael Jackson. That night, kids were all on the dance floor except Sonny. He was a wallflower, standing by himself. I asked him, 'Why don't

you dance?' He said, 'I don't know how.' So I said to him, 'I can't teach the dances that they are dancing out there now, but I can teach you how to slow dance, okay?'"

Sonny and Mrs. Yancey still keep in touch. Last week, on Mrs. Yancey's Facebook page, there was a picture of the Eiffel Tower in the background. In the foreground, it was Sonny, down on his knee with a woman leaning over him. In the next picture, his girlfriend showed her surprised expression with a beautiful ring on her finger. Mrs. Yancey responded to Sonny on Facebook,

"Way to go! Sonny! Congratulations!"

I wondered how she first got involved with foreign exchange students. Listening to Sarah's stories during our afternoon tea time, I gained even more admiration for what she had accomplished.

What is AFS?

American Field Service was established in 1914 by A. Piatt Andrew, a Harvard University Economics Professor and former U.S. Assistant Secretary of the Treasury Stephen Galatti in World War II. The program originally started as a service of volunteer ambulance drivers. Since then, AFS has evolved into an international youth exchange for students. Now the program has more than 50 nonprofit partner countries. Through Sarah's experiences and explanation, I learned about AFS for the first time in my life. Sarah said;

What is AFS's fundamental purpose?

"AFS is an international, voluntary, non-government, non-profit organization. Each year, AFS programs in 103 countries, provide intercultural learning opportunities to help students and adults develop the knowledge, skills, and understanding needed to create a more just and peaceful world. Hosts are needed for foreign exchange students

from other countries. Hosting responsibilities last from a few weeks to a whole year."

With AFS, Sarah became involved in two fully-funded scholarship programs. One program is with the U.S. Department of State through the Bureau of Educational and Cultural Affairs called Future Leader Exchange (FLEX) with countries of the former USSR. The other program is Youth Exchange and Study (YES). YES is for exchange students from primarily Muslim countries. Sarah has been actively involved with AFS programs for 35 years.

We Had Missed The Mark!

Sarah spoke about YES and why it means so much to her.

"The Youth Exchange and Study program started as a result of the tragedies from September 11th. The attacks were horrific. But 9/11 showed that we had missed the mark. We didn't have enough understanding of countries with a significant Muslim population. Since then, lots of money and energy have been directed and devoted to improving levels of understanding and exchange between the U.S. and countries with Muslim populations. Pakistan is one of them. After YES began, I decided to take the students from Pakistan."

Pakistan

In 2013, Mrs. Yancey volunteered to host a girl from Pakistan. Her reasons for choosing this special person were impressive.

"The more I read through her application, the more I liked her. Her name is Fatima. She is a very smart, genuine girl who was born in a village near the Afghan border but she had grown up in Peshawar where she experienced horrific attacks on a school just one year ago. Her mother was a very traditional and conservative woman who was in an arranged marriage at the age of eleven. Fatima's father was killed when she was

only eight months old. At the time of her application, she had won a YES scholarship and wanted to come to the U.S."

Mrs. Yancey "met" Fatima's mother on Skype just one week before Fatima was scheduled to come to the U.S. Her brother translated for their mother; she completely supported her daughter.

"Through our conversations, I realized Fatima was the most motivated of all the candidates. Her primary goal was to show us that not everybody in Pakistan is a terrorist. During conversations on Skype, I assured her family that we were delighted to welcome Fatima and I would take care of her as if she were my own daughter."

When Fatima first arrived, before they even got to Mrs. Yancey's house, Fatima looked completely frightened. She told Mrs.Yancey that her mother wanted her to help Mrs. Yancey with her housework. Mrs. Yancey quickly responded to her:

"'No, no, you did not come here to help me with my work. You came to get an education and learn about America.' She also told me that her mother could tell that I was a good person."

Sarah selected this Pakistani teenager to live in her house for ten months. Some of her neighbors thought she was crazy. Sarah's motivation, however, represents the fundamental American spirit! In my opinion, there is no other country that inherently supports democratic beliefs. Sarah explained to me:

*"My thinking was always like this: **If a student has the courage to think about the impact of an opportunity to experience America and to allow others to get to know her, I will give her that chance**. It seems like a simplistic ideal, but the effect can be life-changing. That kind of kid has a bigger dream about what she wants to do and what she thinks she can accomplish. I had this spontaneous and deep sense of connection with this young girl. A higher power or desire pulled me to do this. Then, I talked with my husband about it. He said, 'if you want to, I will support you.' ..."*

In order to host a student from Pakistan, Sarah and her husband made some changes to their lives. For ten months, they both ate only Kosher meat and no pork. While attending High School in St. Louis county, this young Pakistani girl wore the loose scarf around her head for few weeks and then stopped wearing it. However, she never exposed her arms or legs, though, even when she swam.

Before coming to America, she had never been in a coed school nor been taught by male teachers; or even conversed with a man. She had been taught to say nothing to men. When a man asked a question, she would only say "yes" or "no."

"...She was very, very frightened at first, but she was an incredibly brave kid and tried everything...When she arrived in Washington D.C. and was on the bus with other Pakistan students, the students were stunned to notice that our American bus driver was a woman. All of the Pakistan students were totally in shock especially Fatima! " Sarah added one more example.

The Role of Principal

After teaching honors and regular English for 11 years, Sarah pursued an opportunity to be Assistant Principal at Parkway South High. She explained to me about what the role of principal is about.

"I believe that the responsibility of a principal is to demonstrate how he or she treats students, teachers, and parents. A principal sets the tone, morale, and spirit. Principals are driven to achieve."

Dr. Wayne Mosher was the principal who interviewed Sarah. He asked her one significant question: Where and what were her experiences with young African- American students. Apparently, Sarah's answer was one of the reasons that she was offered the position, which she held for thirteen years. She said;

"My greatest learning was in my first year of teaching. That was when I was asked to be the mentor for African-American students after I finished my internship for a Master's Degree at the University of Virginia."

Mrs. Yancey was assigned to a middle school in St. Louis. At that time, it was the first year of reverse desegregation and a few hundred white students were bused into an all black neighborhood. About 270 white seventh and eighth grade students were assigned to the school. She was stunned! It was the year of 1966-1967.

Desegregation Program

She recalled her first teaching job. *"Here I was, a southern girl who grew up in Virginia and went to school in North Carolina. Our school's corps of teachers included one young Jewish guy from the Bronx, a young Mississippi prim-and-proper black girl, and a Black woman who was ready to retire; the Black woman became my mentor."*

One thing from that first year that stuck in her mind was something her mentor said.

*"... 'If you come here to help our young black students, you should hold high standards for them. Do not have a double standard because you feel sorry for them. You should be tough on them. Spend as much time as you can helping them. Do not let them get away with a thing. **The most important thing you have to do is to let them know that you love them. They know in an instant whether you care about them or not.** If they know you care about them, they will do anything for you.' ...I will never forget that...I worked like a dog at my first teaching job as as English teacher there."*

That year, Mrs. Yancey taught a modernized version of West Side Story. She converted the characters into African-American kids in the hood instead of Puerto Rican and Caucasian kids. They didn't have enough costumes, so they wore black skirts and blue jeans.

Seeds Planted in College

Mrs. Yancey graduated from St. Andrews Presbyterian College (SAPC) in North Carolina. "Christianity and Culture" was the core curriculum for four years. They studied literature, history, philosophy, art, music, and religion.

SPAC decided to send one of its students to participate in a summer program organized by American University. Sarah was that student. In 1964, she and twenty-nine other students from across the country visited Bulgaria, Rumania, East Berlin, Hungary, Czechoslovakia, Yugoslavia, and the Soviet Union.

For two months, thirty students traveled in these countries and gathered information comparing Christianity and Communism. This experience changed her view of the world and her mindset.

The cities of Tashkent, Samarkand and Bukhara made the deepest impression on her. Those cities are located in what is now known as Uzbekistan.

Uzbekistan Student

As part of the Parkway AFS exchange program, there was a struggling student from Uzbekistan. Igor stayed with the Yancey's family one weekend. She asked;

"Do you know I have been in your country, Uzbekistan?"

"You did? Mrs. Yancey!"

"I have been in your city, Tashkent, the capital of your country!"

His eyes popped out and said:

*"No American that I know of has ever come to my country! I can't believe this! I can't believe this! But, **you** came to my city."*

Mrs. Yancey told him that she still had the slides of his hometown. The American Assistant Principal and the Uzbekistan student searched the storage room for the slides taken thirty years ago. With the old projector, they went through them all, one by one. The one that stood out most to Igor was Mrs. Yancey standing by a bridge in the park. Igor couldn't believe what he saw and was touched beyond words. Igor excitedly suggested that Mrs. Yancey make a poster and put it in her school office.

Igor went back to his country and continued on to college. They still stay in touch. A recent email from him was titled, *"Correct English."* He still needs Mrs. Yancey's advice for things like editing English.

Sarah's personal thoughts

* *The problems we have now in the world are not easy to change, but changes do take place.**The future leaders are going to lead us in different directions. The leaders are our young people.***

* ***What is the unifying element in a culturally diverse democracy?** **That is the big and rich question**. That is the question the American and Russian students tried to answer during the exchange in 1995.*

* ***The United States has lots of ethnic groups.** All of them have their own art, history, museum, literature, cuisines, fashion, and moral values. Yet, look at how we manage to come together over 200 years to make our democracy.*

* ***What do we need?** As an educator myself, I think we need more opportunities for young people to know each other, and to think about other countries that have totally different views from ours. Each time you think about it, it gets broader and broader.*

* ***What are the obstacles?** One of them is simply to get enough people to listen, and to find out people who can open their houses to share with exchange students.*

Commonalities:

Other than Pakistan, Uzbekistan, and Russia, Sarah has hosted students from France, Greek Cyprus, India, Norway, Philippines, and Japan. Each student stayed at her house from just three weeks up to one year.

I asked her what she learned from these unique experiences. Her answer surprised me:

"There are distinct differences among us, but there are a lot of commonalities. **One basic fundamental similarity is motherhood. A mother is a mother.** *Mothers love their children. All mothers are concerned about their children's safety, health, happiness, and future success.* **No matter the color of your skin, the language you speak, the religion you believe, if you are a mother, you are in."**

She gave an example:

"Fatima's mother and I have never met in person. We 'met' each other by Skype for only five minutes. It was almost an instant case of Fatima's mother transferring her trust to me and depending on me for all manner of support and advice."

My respect and admiration for Sarah continues to grow. I wondered what the foreign exchange students have learned from her. She shared with me a response from *Sonny.*

"Being fourteen years old and having never traveled outside of the country, my travel to Russia represented a coming-of-age experience. **Leaving my comfort zone and heading to a new country, I discovered a lot about myself and found a whole new perspective on life**. *In* **my interactions with my host family and the people I met, I quickly learned the differences in cultures. It is my desire to continue learning about others in this world that we live in**: *It has fueled my passion to continue traveling."*

Today, Sonny is 36 years old and works for J.P. Morgan Chase Escrow Services in Los Angeles.

What about **_Fatima_**?

"*Before she came to America, her dream was to become doctor. But now, after experiencing a new culture, she is interested in becoming a diplomat. On the last day before Fatima left America to return to her country, she wrote a letter.*

As Chinese old sayings:
*   **A book is like a garden carried in the pocket. A Child's life is like a piece of paper on which every person leaves a mark.**
*   **If you plan for one year, plant rice. If you plan for ten years, plant trees. If you plan for 100 years, educate mankind.**

Postscript:

Sarah and her husband Bob established a "**_World Peace through Higher Learning_**" scholarship fund, raising $15,000 each year to supplement the funding given to Fatima by the college. She is the first recipient of this scholarship designated for international students. In addition, Sarah now spends an increasing amount of time in the St. Louis area working with Interfaith Partnership to bring people from various faith backgrounds together.

The Renaisance Man

Dr. Martin Bell

Fifteen minutes before my cooking class began, I could always expect to see the Bells. This loving couple, Linda and Martin Bell, always came together and arrived early so they could get the best seat, right in the front. Martin, the perfect gentleman, always pulled out the chair for his wife, and then sat on Linda's left. With her sparkling green eyes and sunny smile, Linda's sweet face certainly did cheer me up while I was scrambling during my last-minute class preparation. While we two women chitchatted, Martin read. One time, after having set aside my cleaver on the cutting board, my curiosity kicked in and I asked him what he was reading.

"Oh, it is just magazines and newspaper I read regularly."

He nonchalantly closed his paper, *The New York Times*. From that day on, his reading material appeared on my radar and included reading material from *The Economist Commentary*, *Harvard Journal of Law and Public Policy* to *Opera News* and *Great Operatic Disasters* by Hugh Vickers just to name a few. I made an almost politically incorrect assumption that he must be either a politician or an opera singer.

Politician?

He might be our locally homegrown politician, I thought. When I asked, to my surprise, his response was less complicated, but still profound.

"Being an American, I am very interested in what is going on in our government."

"Why?"

"Because I want to understand how it affects people - the average citizen."

"So, are you a politician?"

"No, not a politician." he shook his head, a small grin showing on his humble face.

"So, what are you?"

"A pediatric surgeon." Unexpectedly, his identity was revealed. But in my mind, I was still very curious to know whether he used to be an opera singer.

Pediatric Surgeon!

Looking at my 3" x 8" cleaver, which I frequently used to demonstrate how to pound, slice, chop and mince pieces of chicken or pork in my cooking class, I wondered what the ultimate requirement was for becoming a surgeon. A pediatric surgeon is responsible for saving newborn babies and children's lives, for sure. One day, when I asked, Martin gave me a short but precise response.

"Skill and judgment."

His answer seemed so simple. Yet, like many apparently simple comments, there was great depth and color reflected in them. For Dr. Bell, skill and judgment are intrinsically connected as one feeds and nurtures the other. The two are blended to form a better one. It took the passing of more years before I came to understand how that happened.

Years later, he mentioned the required skills to become a surgeon during a casual conversation: **precision and delicacy; decisiveness with care.** How was this accomplished? He said he played the piano to achieve delicate movement in both hands. In his 40s, he took ten years of private piano lessons to enhance the skill of his left hand. It was none other than Leonard Slatkin who advised him to do so. Leonard Slatkin? Our famous Leonard Slatkin? The conductor of the St. Louis Symphony recommended it to Dr. Bell, a pediatric surgeon, personally? Seriously?

Yes, indeed. Dr. Bell is a classic music enthusiast, especially opera.

Opera

Dr. Bell loves opera with a passion. Thinking of opera, Puccini's "*Madam Butterfly*" was the only one that I could recall. When I asked him for the name of his all-time favorite opera, secretly I hoped he would answer "*Madame Butterfly.*"

"*You mean just one?...Oh, it is impossible to name just one...but, if I have to choose only one.... Let me think...*" He paused for a long time, before finally replying,

"*There are too many good ones. The earlier operas are about kings, queens and gods...they are mythical, historical or whimsical or allegorical... But what I truly like are the ones from the 19th century, such as La Bohème, Cavalleria Rusticana... Pagliacci...because they deal with the truth. They deal with verismo.*" I had never heard that word before.

"*What is that word you just said?*" I asked.

Verismo

"*Verismo. It refers to a style of Italian opera, which is characterized by its reality and sometimes violence...usually it is about ordinary*

213

people, commoners or lower classes, but the stories are associated with Romanticism.... very emotional...very powerful...it focuses on musical passion and opera singers would beef up their voice on top of their notes in order to accentuate the emotion.... Italy has the best opera!!!"

His broad smile couldn't hide his verismo, his love of Italian opera. Like opera singers enhancing themselves to perform with great emotion, Dr. Bell recognized that building skill and judgment create more opportunities for verismo in life.

His enthusiasm while explaining Italian opera instantly brought back a childhood memory. When I was ten, I would sneak into my father's private collection of classical music records, each as thick as an encyclopedia, while he was at work. Listening to *"Madame Butterfly"* over and over again, I didn't understand what the two opera singers were crying and screaming about, nor did I ever figure out why it was my father's favorite opera. But, I sensed his passion.

Dr. Bell's passion for music stemmed from his upbringing. His father, a violinist, was accepted to the Juilliard School of Music in New York. Unfortunately, his family could not afford for him to pursue his dream. Dr. Bell was influenced by his father's love for violin and played violin during his pre-teen years. However, he never dreamed about majoring in music like his father. He gave a simple reason:

"I am just not good at playing musical instrument; but I've enjoyed and appreciated music all my life."

He nodded humbly, as did Linda, who was sitting next to him. Rightfully so -- she is a pianist herself. She studied at the public High School of Music and Art and later majored in English literature. She studied viola four years at Hunter College in New York. This loving couple obviously shares the same passion for music.

One day in their kitchen, Linda and I reminisced about our childhoods. They reflect two very different worlds. Looking at their kitchen, one wall was shelved with international cookbooks that Linda uses to prepare food. On the wall adjacent to the living room, I noticed all the beautiful, artistic needlework that Linda created and art from places they have traveled around the world. Linda provides a warm and loving environment in their home. Looking outside her kitchen, I saw a small statue of a smiling Buddha and Japanese lanterns in their garden. At that precise moment, I realized that Dr. Bell and I actually had a lot in common.

World Traveler

They are also interested in different cultures, as well as world history. Traveling to various parts of world has become their way of exploring and spending time together. They've toured all over the world: Russia, Eastern Europe, Western Europe, Scandinavia, and the Mediterranean. They've also made three trips to China. One of them was mainly to visit orphanages and children's hospitals in Beijing. In 2008, Dr. Bell made a very special trip to Vietnam. He wanted Linda to see where he served in the military from 1965-1966 during the war. The latest trip was his first trip back to Saigon since after the Vietnam War.

Vietnam War

The trip to Vietnam in 2008 was a poignant one for Dr. Bell. It was the place near Saigon where he served his duty as an American doctor in the army to save soldiers, including Americans, Vietnamese and even Chinese. But, how was a pediatric surgeon serving in the Vietnam War? The stories he shared with me were my first time hearing such experiences. There was always something for me to learn from him each time we met. But I only heard about his experience if I asked a specific question because he is such a humble man.

People in Taiwan viewed the American troops as heroes during the Vietnam War. America sent troops to help democratic South Vietnam fight against the invasion of the Communist North Vietnam. I arrived in America in the late 60's to see the war protesters who were mostly young college students, mostly dressed like hippies and mostly pot smokers marching against American government. I had total culture shock.

I was not prepared to see with my own eyes that ordinary American citizens were openly shouting and screaming in front of the White House. It was my first experience with the meaning of "democracy." At that moment, I understood the meaning of democracy. It meant being able to express the opposite opinions of the government by protesting legally and openly. Dr. Bell said,

"At the beginning of the war, there was not a big controversy until the casualties increased...

...I, myself, did not have any negative feelings about the war. I was completely focused on saving wounded soldiers. Come to think about it, I might have even saved some Chinese - the enemy...

...We went back for the first time after the war. This trip, I just wanted Linda to see it, especially Saigon. The hospital where I served was in Bien Hoa, about fifteen miles from Saigon. Many of the same hotels and restaurants are still there from the 1960s. It was Linda's first trip to Vietnam. It is still a very pretty place, with jungles, flowers and vegetations. Now there are more modern buildings and more business than in the 60s. But it's still a beautiful country."

Different Religions, Common Experiences

I am a proud Chinese; likewise, Linda and Dr. Bell are proud of their Jewish heritage. Because of our common interests and mutual respect, we have attended each other's cultural events. The Bells have come to my cooking classes, and they certainly have taught me enormously about the American spirit. Each time we meet, there is always something for me to learn.

The Bells and I have been close friends for more than a decade. Among the three of us, our friendship has grown into a sibling-hood: like brother and sister. Together, we celebrate Chinese and Jewish holidays. Wearing Chinese red silk jackets, they always come together and joyfully show up fifteen minutes early at the Chinese restaurant. This is for my annual Chinese New Year Party to observe the Lion Dance and listen to my brief introduction of the symbol each year before the twelve-course dinner. Reciprocally, I have been invited to share Passover Seder at their house. Since Linda is few years older than I am, according to our tradition, I respectfully call her "Jie Jie" in Chinese, which means big sister. One year, Linda (Jie Jie) asked me to bring two roasted ducks, cut into smaller pieces for their Passover. As her younger Chinese sister, I was honored to do exactly as my big sister requested. As usual, eighteen guests sat around a long rectangular table in their dining room. Dr. Bell spoke briefly about the meaning of the Passover celebration. Each guest took turns reading and following the sixteen pages of passages from the, Haggadah, Order of the Passover Seder. We all participated in the rituals: washing our hands, reciting the Kiddush, breaking the matzah, eating bitter vegetables dipped in salt water as well as eating other symbolic dishes.

In between, Dr. Bell and his family members, including his son Adam and granddaughter, Samantha, would read in Hebrew. We respect each other's cultural traditions, as well as how history has shaped us into who we are today.

New York! New York!

How does Dr. Bell stay so open and curious to cultures and ideas? This New Yorker shared his blend of stimuli.

"To me, New York is a large university. There is so much to see, learn, and do in New York...the city itself is exciting -- you get to see Broadway shows, museums, art galleries, Chinatown, and visit our old friends. We see all kinds of people on the street, taste different cuisines from different countries... There's lots of energy...When I am back home in St. Louis, I read..."

"Any specific books you like to read these days?" I was curious.

"Since I love history, historical fiction is my favorite, like 'Portrait of an Unknown Woman by Vanora Bennett....

... The story is about Sir Thomas Moore's dear and friends in the 16th century. Also, one of my favorite authors is Clive Cussler. His books are adventure or science fiction, like 'The Silent Sea' and the 'Foundation' series by Isaac Asimov...

... I also find Montessori education very interesting! Italian physician and educator Maria Montessori developed it. She emphasized independence, freedom within limits, and respect for a child's natural psychological development, as well as technological advancements. In Italy, Montessori education serves children from birth to eighteen years old..."

Being a teacher myself, I couldn't agree more with Montessori's belief in fundamental education, but Dr. Bell was a physician and professor before his retirement. Why his interest now in education? He gave me another one word answer: "Docent." It is what he is doing now.

Docent!

"What is that?" Another new vocabulary word I learned from Dr. Bell.

"A docent is a volunteer teacher or lecturer at various institutions, like museums, zoos and our opera theater...

... I am involved with the Life Long Institute at Washington University for people over 55 years old who want to study opera, politics, Italian culture and other subjects... There are many retired professionals who exchange ideas and knowledge, I am one of them. As a docent of opera, I teach at senior retirement centers. I give talks about specific operas, the composers, and the background. The operas I choose are usually popular ones."

At that moment, I was in deep thought, thinking we both have retired from professional career. My work for thirty eight years was teaching at a public high school, where there is only one boss above the teachers -- the principal. He was physician. All of a sudden, I was very curious about what the boss was called at a hospital, the equivalent of my high school's principal, so I asked Dr. Bell.

"*Chief of Staff.* " He answered. Then I found out that Dr. Bell **was** the Chief of Staff at St. John's Mercy Medical Center during his last six years of work before he retired. It was the first time I had heard his job title even though we had been friends more than ten years. What a humble man!

Being a defiant, anti-authority person myself, I can't imagine what it is like to be the head of a medical staff. So I presented my question.

"*How do you adjust to life after being in such a lofty position?*"

The answer he gave me reflects his strong belief about the essence of retirement.

"*It is not where you retire from; it is where you retire to!*"

Dr. Bell is a true Renaissance man, enlightened, multi-faceted, and humble.

As Chinese old sayings:
* *He knows most who speaks least.*
* *A single conversation with a wise man is better than ten years of study.*
* *If there is beauty in character, there will be harmony in the home. If there is a harmony in the home, there will be order in the nation. If there is order in the nation, there will be peace in the world.*